# FASHION REIMAGINED

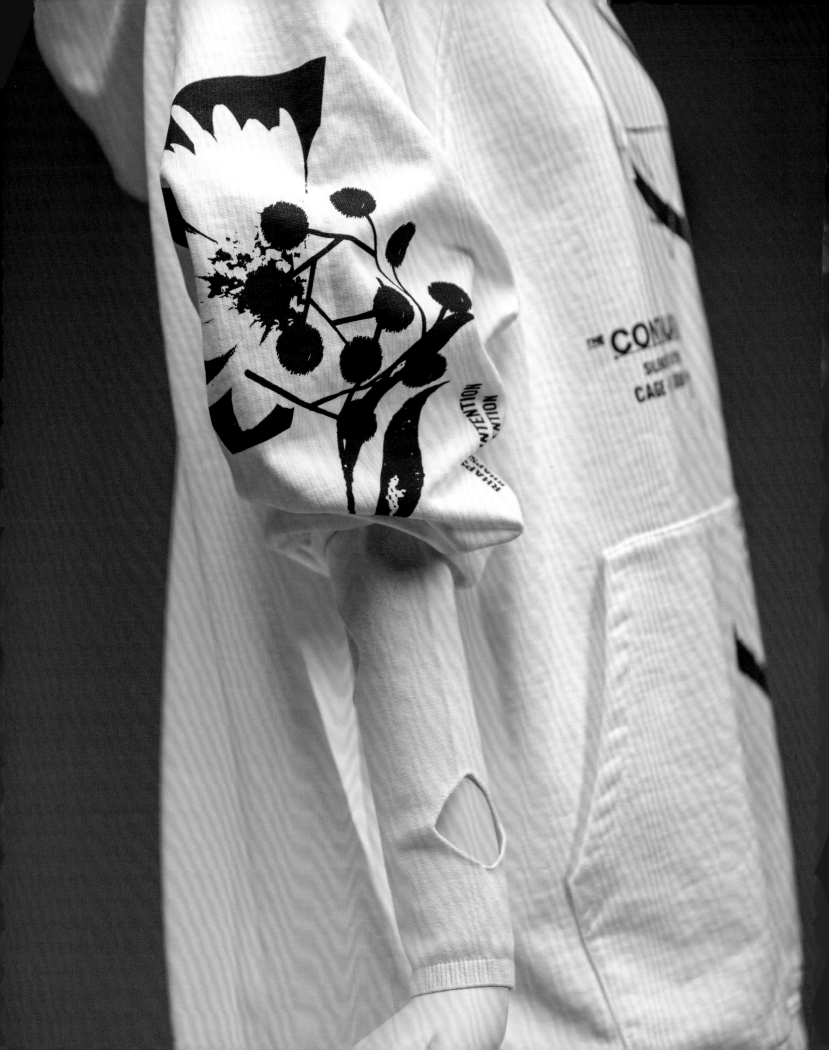

# FASHION REIMAGINED

## THEMES AND VARIATIONS, 1760–NOW

Annie Carlano

Lauren D. Whitley

Ellen C. Walker Show

Anna Sui

The Mint Museum
in association with D Giles Limited

This book was published in conjunction with the exhibition *Fashion Reimagined: Themes and Variations 1760–Now*, organized by The Mint Museum, Charlotte, North Carolina, December 10, 2022–June 18, 2023

Mint Museum Uptown at Levine Center for the Arts
500 South Tryon Street
Charlotte, North Carolina 28202
www.mintmuseum.org

Copyright © 2022 Mint Museum of Art, Inc.
First published in 2022 by GILES
An imprint of D Giles Limited
60 High Street
Lewes, BN7 1XG, UK
gilesltd.com

ISBN (hardcover): 978-1-913875-16-9

*Fashion Reimagined: Themes and Variations 1760–Now* is presented with generous support from Wells Fargo Wealth & Investment Management; additional support from the Mint Museum Auxiliary and Bank OZK.

The Mint Museum is supported, in part, by the Infusion Fund and its generous donors; the North Carolina Arts Council, a division of the Department of Cultural Resources; the City of Charlotte; and its members.

Library of Congress Cataloging-in-Publication Data

Names: Carlano, Annie, author. | Show, Ellen C. Walker, author. | Whitley, Lauren D., author. | Sui, Anna, author. | Mint Museum (Charlotte, N.C.), sponsoring body, host institution.
Title: Fashion reimagined : themes and variations 1760-now / Annie Carlano, Lauren D. Whitley, Ellen C. Walker Show, Anna Sui.
Description: Charlotte, North Carolina : The Mint Museum; London : D Giles Ltd, 2022. | "This book was published in conjunction with the exhibition Fashion Reimagined: Themes and Variations 1760-NOW, organized by The Mint Museum, Charlotte, North Carolina, December 10, 2022 - June 18, 2023." | Includes bibliographical references. | Summary: "This book was published in conjunction with the exhibition Fashion Reimagined: Themes and Variations 1760 - NOW, organized by The Mint Museum, Charlotte, North Carolina"-- Provided by publisher.
Identifiers: LCCN 2022016756 | ISBN 9781913875169 (hardcover)
Subjects: LCSH: Mint Museum (Charlotte, N.C.)--Catalogs. | Fashion--History--Exhibitions. | Clothing and dress--History--Exhibitions.
Classification: LCC TT502 .C375 2022 | DDC 746.9/207475676--dc23/eng/20220803
LC record available at https://lccn.loc.gov/2022016756

For D Giles Limited:
Copy-edited and proof-read by Jenny Wilson
Designed by Ocky Murray
Produced by GILES, an imprint of D Giles Limited
Printed and bound in China

Front cover: Iris van Herpen (Netherlands, 1984–) "Labyrinthine" dress from "Sensory Seas" collection Spring/Summer 2020

Back cover: Unknown makers (England, 18th century) Formal dress, sack-back open robe and petticoat, 1760s–80s

# CONTENTS

# FOREWORD

ashion is so much more than just clothes. For centuries, artists who have designed garments as protection from the elements, or to communicate cultural identity or station in life, have done so through many processes and skill sets needed to robe and adorn the body. Raw materials for the cloth must be found and gathered, fabric woven, felted, or created in some way, and pattern pieces for the desired shapes calculated and sewn together to make the desired silhouette. What we choose to wear when we get up each morning, how we express ourselves, has great impact on how we feel, and how others feel about us.

Reflecting attitudes about health, beauty, status, philosophy, architecture, art, and design of the time in which it is created, fashion is coded with symbolic features perhaps more than any other visual art—if only due to its ubiquitous nature as part of our everyday lives! Historically established at court, in a trickledown effect, today the increased democratization of the latest trends often comes from the street up, or from off the beaten track. In recent years, fashion designers have embraced sustainability and social responsibility in the making of clothing and in their business practices, ahead of other industries.

Anyone who has lived through multiple decades has had the experience of witnessing certain fashion trends reemerge that remind them of the clothes they wore in their youth. This is not simply rehashing early styles, but a kind of evolution that pays homage to the innovations and innovators of the past and reimagines them to become part of a new voice to reflect and serve our contemporary world.

*Fashion Reimagined: Themes and Variations 1760–NOW* is an exhibition drawn entirely from the illustrious holdings of The Mint Museum. It has been organized to celebrate the fiftieth anniversary of the founding of the costume and textile collection in 1972 by the Mint Museum Woman's Auxiliary. Looking at the collection through three pervasive themes throughout four centuries of dress, the impact of historicism on contemporary fashion, even the most avant-garde designs, is apparent. Starting with "Minimalism," the focus is on the line, the purity of the contour, with little embellishment. The "Pattern and Decoration" section illustrates emphasis on color, motifs, and texture. Extension, exaggeration, or transformative approaches to the body are featured in the third section, "The Body Reimagined."

Selecting highlights from thousands of fashions, carrying out research, conservation, and other preparations of the men's and women's garments, matching or modifying mannequins to each garment, padding and creating undergarments to create the precise armature for the silhouette, and preparation of this book, was a tremendous undertaking. Annie Carlano, Senior Curator of Craft, Design & Fashion and curator of the exhibition, has my thanks for conceiving the idea for the show, and for her insistence on scholarly excellence in both written word and presentation. Ellen C. Walker Show, Director of Library & Archives, and guest author Lauren D. Whitley have ably contributed their expertise and insights. I am also enormously grateful to fashion designer Anna Sui, who has written an intimate prologue from the maker's point of view, setting the tone for the book.

The Mint Museum Auxiliary has my profound appreciation for their many contributions to The Mint Museum over the years, but especially for founding and building the fashion collection.

I am deeply grateful to Wells Fargo Wealth & Investment Management, generous lead sponsors of *Fashion Reimagined*, and to Jay Everette, Community Relations Manager, Wells Fargo Social Impact, for his ongoing support of important fashion initiatives at the Mint. A profound thank you to the Mint Museum Auxiliary, and Liz Shuford, President, for literally making this exhibition and book possible through extraordinary philanthropy, acquisitions, and sponsorship.

As a former Arkansan, I am pleased for the opportunity to partner with sponsors Bank OZK and much appreciate their support of *Fashion Reimagined*.

Todd A. Herman PhD
President & CEO

# SPONSOR'S STATEMENT

"A couturier must be an architect for design, a sculptor for shape, a painter for color, a musician for harmony, and a philosopher for temperance."

Cristóbal Balenciaga

Wells Fargo is honored to support the presentation of *Fashion Reimagined*. The exhibition highlights 50 signature fashions drawn entirely from The Mint Museum's permanent collection. The exhibition also celebrates the 50th anniversary of the founding of the museum's "costume collection" and honors the Mint Museum Auxiliary's role in the founding of, and continued contributions to, the collection. Through its thematic exploration of Minimalism, Pattern and Decoration, and the Body Reimagined, the exhibition brings to life Balenciaga's assessment of the fashion designer's challenges and the creative skill of their craft. We celebrate the mission and work of The Mint Museum in preserving and presenting these works to the public.

**Jay Everette**
Community Relations Manager,
Wells Fargo Social Impact

# PROLOGUE

Designing a fashion collection is always a challenge. You pray for divine intervention. You hope you have an idea, theme, or concept that can be expounded. The idea can spark from a movie, photograph, book, TV show; just about anything. But the idea has to be relevant. There must be something that will relate to *now*.

One of the few times I did a collection that was influenced by the moment was the grunge collection, Spring 1993. There was incredible music coming from Seattle and other cities across the US: Nirvana, Pearl Jam, Smashing Pumpkins, Alice In Chains, Mazzy Star, to name a few. And there was a very distinct, new style: plaid shirts, knit caps, layering, Dr. Martens.

Most collections were conjured from a glimpse of something alluring, and I began researching the subject. I remember watching a Busby Berkeley movie, *Gold Diggers of 1933*, with my dad. Loving all the rehearsal outfits on the dancers as they were practicing their steps, I researched more of Berkeley's movies; in fact, I bought a box set of his films. The 1930s fashions had very fluid bias cuts, and the short rehearsal clothes reminded me of the "hot pants" from the 1970s. This became my Spring 2008 collection.

Sometimes there is an artist that inspires me. In the case of Naiad and Walter Einsel, there were two. They were a husband-and-wife team who illustrated for magazines, newspapers, and ads from the 1950s to the 1970s. I just loved their style. Naiad had a very specific dotted line quality, similar to Andy Warhol's early drawings. She began at *Seventeen* magazine and eventually went to the *New York Times*.

But her commercial art was very prominent. She became art director at CBS and her husband, Walter, held the same position at NBC. I became so obsessed with their work that I sought out Naiad and went to visit her home in Westport, Connecticut. It was so awe-inspiring to see how their whole environment reflected their aesthetics. Naiad also published a book of their yearly valentines to each other. Her unique style incorporated rubber stamps into line drawings. Walter loved working in wood, so his valentines were carved in an American Folk Art manner, usually articulated. Inspired by their mid-century, American Folk Art style, I created my Fall 2012 collection.

Other collections have been inspired by my days of dreaming of becoming a fashion designer. Growing up in Detroit, I loved *Seventeen* magazine and eventually *Vogue*, *Mademoiselle*, and *Glamour*. The fashions featured in these magazines were available at J. L. Hudson. Being able to see them in person was a big thrill. My first collection, Fall 1991, was inspired by the August back-to-school issue of *Seventeen* magazine. The influence of mod and pop was very prevalent, and I particularly loved the black and white houndstooth worn with bright colored vinyl. My recent Fall 2022 collection also featured a lot of the same inspiration, with an added focus coming from a documentary about *Ready Steady Go!*, a weekly British music and dance party TV show from the 1960s. It featured new bands like the Rolling Stones, the Beatles, and the Who. There was a hostess, Cathy McGowan, who wore the latest mod fashions by Mary Quant and Foale & Tuffin. I was so inspired by the TV show that we made a video to present the collection that looked like a segment of the show. And we accompanied it with Generation X's (Billy Idol's) song "Ready Steady Go."

Perhaps my favorite collections have been inspired by a mashup of personal influences. I started Spring 2007 inspired by the fashions of Marie Antoinette. My friend Sofia Coppola was filming her movie in Paris, and I was lucky to be able to visit the set. The fabrics I selected were pastel colors in brocades, jacquards, and taffetas. In the middle of working on the collection I went on vacation to Turkey and saw a great exhibition on Barbarossa the pirate. I always loved the N. C. Wyeth illustration of *Treasure Island*. So, I added black, white, and red stripes which reminded me of the strict dress code of one of my favorite bands, the New York Dolls. Black, red, white, stripes, roses, and polka dots. I mixed this all with some punk styling to create one of my all-time favorite shows.

As you can see, I never know what influences will infiltrate into the collections. Sometimes something inspires the whole collection or sometimes it's just one outfit. But surely, it's always very personal. I collect images that reflect my inspiration and put them all on my inspiration board. The images are selected for invoking the theme but also the color scheme. I arrange the images by color, and this becomes my color story. With my team, I work on fabrics and prints that reflect the board and this helps keep me focused. The board also inspires the other people that work on the runway show: the hair, makeup, accessories, shoes, stockings, jewelry, invitation, even the music collaborators. This way everyone has the same inspiration and can follow along the same graphics and flavor of the board.

I think I have the best job in the world because I can always focus on what I love, what I'm obsessed with at the moment, and learn more about it. Research is my favorite part of the process, and if I can discover what influenced a particular artistic movement, fashion style, or work of art, then it's really rewarding. The discoveries and connections along the way are thrilling.

Anna Sui

# A BRIEF HISTORY OF THE FASHION COLLECTION

## AT THE MINT MUSEUM

**Fig 1** *Fashions 1840–1940* exhibition brochure, 1976.
Costume Committee Scrapbook, Charles L. Mo Collection. Courtesy of The Mint Museum Archives.

Three members of the Mint Museum Woman's Auxiliary are credited with founding the Mint Museum Costume Collection in 1972. Lillian Crosland, Ruth Lucas, and Hannah Withers conceived of the Collection to preserve family heirloom garments of artistic and historic merit. They formed the first Costume Collection Committee of the Woman's Auxiliary and led a group of volunteers in soliciting donations as well as repairing and displaying the donated fashions. In those early days, they accepted all donations of historic men's, women's, and children's clothing. Arthur J. "Pete" Ballard, Curator of the Costume Collection at Reynolda House Museum of American Art in Winston-Salem, North Carolina, and an "antique garment-restorer," advised the Committee on a volunteer basis. He also taught classes in garment restoration to the many volunteers who maintained the burgeoning collection during the 1970s and early 1980s, as well as designing and curating the costume exhibitions with the Costume Committee.

The Mint Museum of Art hosted the first costume exhibition, *Fashions 1840–1940*, in 1976 (Figure 1). This exhibition featured 101 garments and accompanying accessories exclusively from the Mint's collection. The costume volunteers worked with Ballard to prepare, dress, and arrange the mannequins. The Costume Committee also supplied dressed mannequins for displays outside the museum, including several of the annual Woman's Auxiliary Antiques Shows (Figure 2), the 1977 Southern Christmas Show, the 100th anniversary celebration of the Mutual Savings and Loan Association in 1981, and a 1982 Charlotte Symphony post-gala dessert party.

When The Mint Museum of History opened on July 3, 1976, its Historical Fashion Gallery became the main exhibition space for the Costume Collection. Exhibitions, some with evocative titles like *You Bet Your Bloomers* and *Don't Go Near the Water: Bathing Suits Old & New*, continued almost yearly until 1985. Touring exhibitions *Paper Dolls: Children's Clothing* and *Headlines: A Hundred Years of Hats, 1840–1940* (co-sponsored by the Statesville, North Carolina, Arts and Science Museum) also originated at The Mint Museum of History during this period (Figure 3). Pete Ballard, still volunteering his services, was named Associate Curator of Historical Costumes in 1978 to acknowledge his continuing work on these exhibitions and with the Costume Collection. The demanding exhibition schedule required more people to help, so Ballard taught summer-long workshops in garment restoration to recruit and train volunteers from the community. For the first time, membership in the Woman's Auxiliary was not required to participate.

**Fig 2** Costume Collection display at the Mint Museum Antiques Show, 1981.
Costume Committee Scrapbook, Charles L. Mo Collection. Courtesy of The Mint Museum Archives.

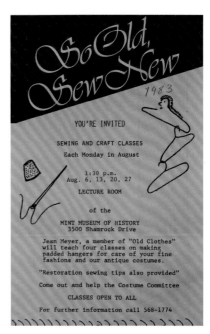

The Costume Committee, supported by the Woman's Auxiliary and the Fashion Group of Charlotte, provided funding for the maintenance, storage, and exhibition of the collection, as well as professional collection appraisals. They also developed the So Old Sew New project, collecting and packaging fabric scraps for resale in the History Museum's gift store to raise funds (Figure 4). Additionally, the Costume Committee applied for and received grants to support exhibitions, and to purchase mannequins for display. One three-year grant from the Mary Duke Biddle Foundation funded a stipend for Pete Ballard and all preparation costs for *The Evolution of Fashion: 1909–1919*, a large exhibition that opened in August 1980 and featured more than 85 garments and accessories from the Costume Collection (Figure 5). The Costume Committee maintained possession of the collection until formally transferring ownership to the museum in 1983–4; the museum budgeted money for collection care for the first time in 1983.

Beginning in the 1970s, the Costume Committee of the Auxiliary rented a space at Spirit Square in uptown Charlotte that doubled as a workshop and storage area. The group met weekly to document and repair garments in the collection. The storage area was too small to accommodate all of the garments and accessories, so items were distributed among several locations in Charlotte. The 1985 expansion of The Mint Museum of Art included designated storage space to accommodate the entire collection (Figure 6). Once the construction of specialized storage units was completed in the Costume Collection and Textile Area, the collection of over 6,000 items was consolidated in 1986 (Figure 7).

Professionalization of the Costume Collection occurred when, through the generosity of an anonymous donor, The Mint Museum

hired its first staff Curator of Costumes, Patricia Roath, in 1987. She inventoried the collection and curated the 1989 inaugural exhibition of The Mint Museum of Art Costume Gallery, *Quiet Grace and Liveliness: Cotton Print Dresses 1825–1865*. Jane Starnes succeeded Roath in 1989. Her tenure included the 1991 acquisition of an early twentieth-century "Delphos" gown designed by Fortuny, purchased with funds from the Costume Committee, significant because it was one of the first gowns purchased for a collection built on donated garments (see Fig 8). The year 1991 was also significant because the museum established Costume as a distinct curatorial department. Jane Starnes remained curator until 1996, when the funding for her position ended with the death of the anonymous donor.

Charles Mo, who had been hired in 1984 as Curator of Fine Arts, and subsequently Director/Vice President of Fine Arts, assumed responsibility for the Historic Costume Collection in 1996. It was later renamed the Historic Costume and Fashionable Dress Collection, as garments by designers including Gabrielle "Coco" Chanel, Pierre Balmain, Christian Dior, Zandra Rhodes, Christian Lacroix, Oscar de la Renta, and Gianni Versace were donated or purchased, chiefly with funds provided by the Mint Museum Auxiliary, under the leadership of Costume Chair Lyn Mack. Working in conjunction with the Costume Committee, Mo dedicated many hours to showcasing the collection and reaching a broader audience. Exhibitions such as *The Art of Affluence:*

**Fig 5a (left)** *The Evolution of Fashion: 1909–1919* mannequins on display, 1980.
Costume Committee Scrapbook, Charles L. Mo Collection. Courtesy of The Mint Museum Archives.

**Fig 5b (right)** *The Evolution of Fashion: 1909–1919* exhibition catalogue, 1980.
Costume Committee Scrapbook, Charles L. Mo Collection. Courtesy of The Mint Museum Archives.

**Fig 6 (left)** The Mint Museum attic space designated for Costume Collection storage during renovation, 1985. (Left to right) Bill McGee, architect; Steve Musgrove, Mint Museum Deputy Director; Milton Bloch, Mint Museum Director.
Costume Committee Scrapbook, Charles L. Mo Collection. Courtesy of The Mint Museum Archives.

**Fig 7 (right)** Custom-built drawers in Costume Storage after renovation, 1986.
Costume Committee Scrapbook, Charles L. Mo Collection. Courtesy of The Mint Museum Archives.

*Haute Couture and Luxury Fashions 1947–2007*, *And the Bead Goes On*, and *The Heights of Fashion: Platform Shoes Then and Now* featured modern dress and reflected the additions of more contemporary garments and accessories to the collection.

Following Charles Mo's retirement in 2013, Annie Carlano, Senior Curator of Craft, Design, & Fashion, accepted the stewardship of what is now called the Fashion Collection, and further advanced best practices in curatorial and conservation. Titi Halle, a costume and textile specialist, thoroughly assessed the collection with Carlano in 2014. Conservator and dresser Tae Smith was contracted to survey, treat, and install. Exhibitions in 2015 highlighted contemporary fashion and international designers, with *Viva Moschino!* and *Body Embellishment*, which included the first art museum installation by the New York-based Israeli, Lebanese/Palestinian, and German/Tajik designers, threeASFOUR. The 2017–18 season was declared "The Year of Fashion," and exhibitions celebrated the Fashion Collection and its supporters. *Charlotte Collects: Contemporary Couture and Fabulous Fashion* featured fashions from the personal collections of Charlotteans, many of whom became part of a Fashion Task Force in support of an enhanced Fashion facility. *The Glamour and Romance of Oscar de la Renta*, curated by André Leon Talley and highlighting pieces from the de la Renta archives, included items from the Mint Museum Fashion Collection and through Auxiliary Costume Chair Marianna Sheridan, archivist at ODLR.

"The Year of Fashion" was also the year an extraordinary transformational gift from generous donors Ann and Michael Tarwater moved the museum to hire Gluckman Tang Architects to conduct a feasibility study on expanding the footprint of the Fashion Collection. Envisioned as a Fashion Studio with spaces for storage,

**Fig 8** *Fortuny: Robed in Riches*
exhibition catalogue, 1992.
Exhibitions Collection Catalogues.
Courtesy of The Mint Museum Archives.

study, immersive programs and exhibitions, the project was still in the developmental phase when it was paused temporarily due to the COVID-19 pandemic.

Despite the disruption, the collection continues to grow, thanks to the ongoing generosity of Deidre and Clay Grubb, who have greatly helped expand holdings of diverse designers, such as Anamika Khanna and Walé Oyéjidé. *The World of Anna Sui* exhibition opened at the Mint in 2021, and that same year an ensemble from her Spring/Summer collection was acquired. Originating as a collection of historic garments from local families, the Fashion Collection at The Mint Museum has evolved to become one of the largest and most important holdings, and to include past and contemporary haute couture clothing, ready-to-wear, accessories, and textiles from around the world.

Ellen C. Walker Show

# CATALOGUE

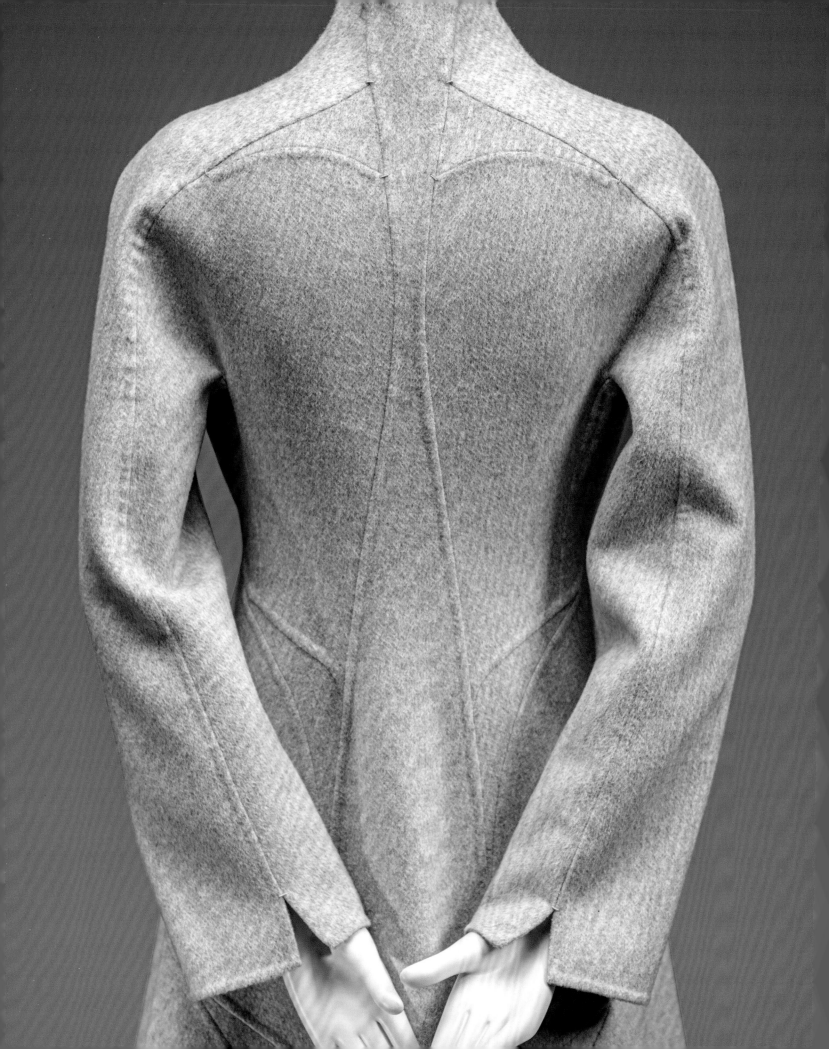

# MINIMALISM

Focused on clean lines and sparse surface decoration, the minimalist approach to fashion design is simple and reductive. The earliest attempts at what we know as clothing probably began as a means of protecting the body from the elements, providing warmth, or shielding the skin from sunburn. From excavations in what is now the Czech Republic we know that humankind created systems for interlacing fibers to create plain weave and open twining as early as 27,000 years ago, for nets. But the earliest known garment dates to the earliest years of the Egyptian Kingdom about 5,000 years ago and is a natural linen sheath with simple construction. Originally decorated, intended to adorn as much as protect, this was high fashion.

It is, however, ancient Greek dress and its minimalist aesthetic, in both its interpretations and reinventions, that has been a pervasive influence in fashion history. Minimal in its construction, high fashion in ancient Greece consisted of two pieces, the tunic and the cloak. Draped on the body, falling in graceful folds to the floor, and fastened with a clasp, the fabric followed the contour of the body. The persistence of this theme in Western fashion, from neo-classicism onwards, is rooted in part in its comfort, but also in its association with woman as goddess. Neo-classical dress itself influenced fashion of the twentieth century in both men's and women's fashions, in terms of cut and fabrics, such as thin muted stripes.

In the United States, the impact of the 1960s and '70s Minimalist art movement influenced certain fashion trends. Looking at dress as a sculptural artform, for certain makers the emphasis was on shapes and contours, geometry, and eschewing bright colors. At the same time here and in Europe, revolutionary cultural forces, the space race, and the youth craze influenced the reduction of hemlines and further interest in simple pattern pieces and basic geometric shapes.

### Gabrielle "Coco" Chanel (France, 1883–1971)
For Chanel. France, founded 1913
Day ensemble: dress and jacket, 1929
Wool jersey, jacquard knit

Gift of the Mint Museum Auxiliary, donated by Mildred Taylor Cook. 1983.75.467a-c

Women's fashions in the first decade of the twentieth century consisted of tight-fitting corsets under long narrow dresses or skirts that hobbled movement. Made of fabrics that were inflexible, such fashions were uncomfortable and designed to objectify women's bodies. Seeking to design clothes for active women, who had entered the work force, rode bicycles, and led busy social lives, Gabrielle Chanel was inspired by menswear and knitted sportswear in her own attire, and expanded her millinery business into a full-fledged womenswear company.

This rare daytime ensemble is an outstanding example of the comfortable modern attire first introduced by Chanel in the 1910s. The soft drape of the knitted dress, with its relatively short hemline, was designed to permit ease of movement. Worn with the relaxed jacket, the ample elongated silhouette is a reductive minimalist design, mostly black. Chanel championed black as the most elegant color for the modern silhouette, as it accentuates the purity of line so important to her fashion designs. Her little black dress, a staple of the modern woman's wardrobe, was flattering and democratic in its relative accessibility for women.

In this ensemble, a limited palette of black and white and a pattern of bands of stripes, chevrons, and small geometric motifs, provide a striking graphic design, not unlike the abstract rhythmic Russian vernacular designs of her earlier 1920s dresses.

Among Chanel's friends was the Georgian artist Ilia Zdanevich, known as Iliazd, himself a friend of painter and textile designer Sonia Delaunay. In 1928 Zdanevich began working for Tissu Chanel, where he brought both his pattern design and engineering skills to combine in new weaving machines that perfected the process of making knit jersey fabrics for Gabrielle Chanel's fashions.

This day ensemble is depicted in the November 9, 1929 issue of *Vogue*, a version of it captured in an illustration by the English court dressmaker Madame Handley-Seymour, now in the collection of the Victoria and Albert Museum in London. AC

**Henriette Negrin (France, 1877–1965)**
**Mariano Fortuny y Madrazo (Spain and Italy, 1871–1949)**
"Delphos" dress, circa 1915–30
Pleated silk plain weave, glass beads, stenciled velvet belt

Gift of the Mint Museum Auxiliary, Purchase Funds Provided by the Costume Collection Committee. 1991.12a-b

Among the most iconic of designs associated with the fashion designer Mariano Fortuny y Madrazo is the "Delphos" dress. Distinguished by long vertical pleats that form an elegant columnar sheath, it was inspired by ancient Greek garments, called *chitons*, as seen on the famous fifth-century BCE bronze sculpture, *The Charioteer of Delphi*. Fortuny deliberately eschewed mainstream fashion trends when creating his classic goddess dress, and the Delphos became a favorite in bohemian artistic circles in the early twentieth century. Marcel Proust perfectly captured the aura of Fortuny dresses in his *Remembrance of Things Past*; Albertine receives several Delphos dresses from her lover, highlighting not only their ability to evoke both a dreamy past and a timeless present, but also their erotic quality.

The original Delphos dress was a sheath of silk that achieved its distinctive look through an innovative method of fine pleating. The exact method was a closely guarded secret involving heat, pressure, and ceramic rods. Later versions of the Delphos featured sleeves and overblouses, again inspired by an ancient form called the *peplos*. While these early forms changed little in the several decades of production that followed, Delphos colors varied and included ice blue, saffron, mushroom, and the pink seen on this sleeveless example. Body-hugging with an elegant pooling of silk at the hem, this dress is finished with Murano Venetian glass bead edging and a stenciled velvet belt, both characteristic Delphos features.

For decades the Delphos was considered the invention of Fortuny alone, and indeed he filed a patent for the design in 1909. However, recent scholarship has established that his partner and later wife, Henriette Negrin, was the actual creator of this iconic garment. Negrin, who had extensive experience as a dressmaker, was recorded by Fortuny as experimenting with various slats and folds in silk to produce the pleats, and he acknowledged her contributions in a side note on the original patent. LDW

**Mary McFadden (United States, 1938–)**
Evening dress, 1980s
Pleated polyester, embroidered with sequins
and glass beads

Gift of Katherine McKay Belk-Cook. 2005.66.4

It can be difficult to date a Mary McFadden dress. Since the 1970s she has been creating timeless and trendless dresses with her own brand of classicism touched with a heavy dose of rich ornamentation. Then, as now, McFadden starts with a pleated sheath dress which acts as a blank canvas for the luxuriously hand-crafted decoration. The many inspirations that have informed her designs over the years have ranged from ancient Greek dresses to Peruvian weavings, and once inspired curator Harold Koda to call McFadden a "design archeologist."

Her path to creating began in Tennessee and wound through summers as a girl in Paris with her grandmother. A marriage in the 1960s brought a move to South Africa and initiated a lifelong passion for travel and appreciation for textiles from around the globe. Many of her finds were transformed into clothing for herself, in what we would acknowledge today as appropriation, but which in the 1970s she viewed as inspiration, and led her to launching Mary McFadden Designs in 1973.

Here, the diaphanous white fabric was achieved by the "Marii" technique, a multi-step process of permanently heat-setting pleats in polyester that McFadden patented in 1975. The simple columnar sheath acts as a foil for the colorful bodice encrusted with sequins and glass beads. With its black and white geometric pattern complemented by swaths of colored and gold beads, it evokes the richness of an Art Nouveau painting by Gustav Klimt but also an exotic bejeweled Byzantine mosaic. McFadden relied on the expertise of artists around the world to develop and execute her wearable art. The skills of Indian artisans informed the rich embroidery and construction of this dress, while artists in Korea and Germany likely participated in the production of the colorful beads, inspired by those McFadden collected on her extensive travels. LDW

**Ermenegildo Zegna S.p.A. (Italy, founded 1910)**
Gentleman's dress suit, 2000
Wool, silk

Gift of Mr. and Mrs. Jonathan B. Simon. 2011.8a-b

The origins of the Ermenegildo Zegna company are in the wool industry. With high mountain pastures and pristine waters ideal for sheep, there has been wool production in the Italian Alps province of Biella since the Middle Ages. In the late nineteenth century, industrialization modernized production, and by 1910 Ermenegildo Zegna (1892–1966) had begun to create fine woolens, from sheep to fabric. Overseeing all aspects of the business, and driven by a goal to make the finest cloth in the world, he and his family were vigilant about every facet of the company, from the quality of the raw materials to textile design, sales, and distribution.

In 1968, under Zegna's sons Aldo and Angelo, the company began to make ready-to-wear men's suits. From the sourcing of the finest merino wool, Kashmir goat hair, and South African kid mohair, to the spinning and plying of yarn, to the dyeing and weaving onsite at the original Zegna mill, all elements of the fabric are luxurious. When the cloth is removed from the loom, it is washed, steamed, brushed by hand, and sent to the factory in Switzerland where it is cut to size and sent on to the factory in Padua for 140-part construction, all by hand, by expert tailors and others, except for a machine that cuts out the winglets for the chest pocket. At every stage the cloth and pattern pieces are checked and rechecked for any imperfections, before being released to exclusive retail venues.

Ermenegildo Zegna S.p.A. was in a strong position to add a made-to-measure line to its luxury brand and, in 1972, Su Misura was established. Competing with couture houses and the best English tailors, the Su Misura process starts with the client's selection of a silhouette and desired Zegna fabrics, including linings, before measurements are taken and the bespoke suit is fitted and made. This suit was custom-made for the donor, the proprietor of a fine men's clothing store in Charlotte, North Carolina. AC

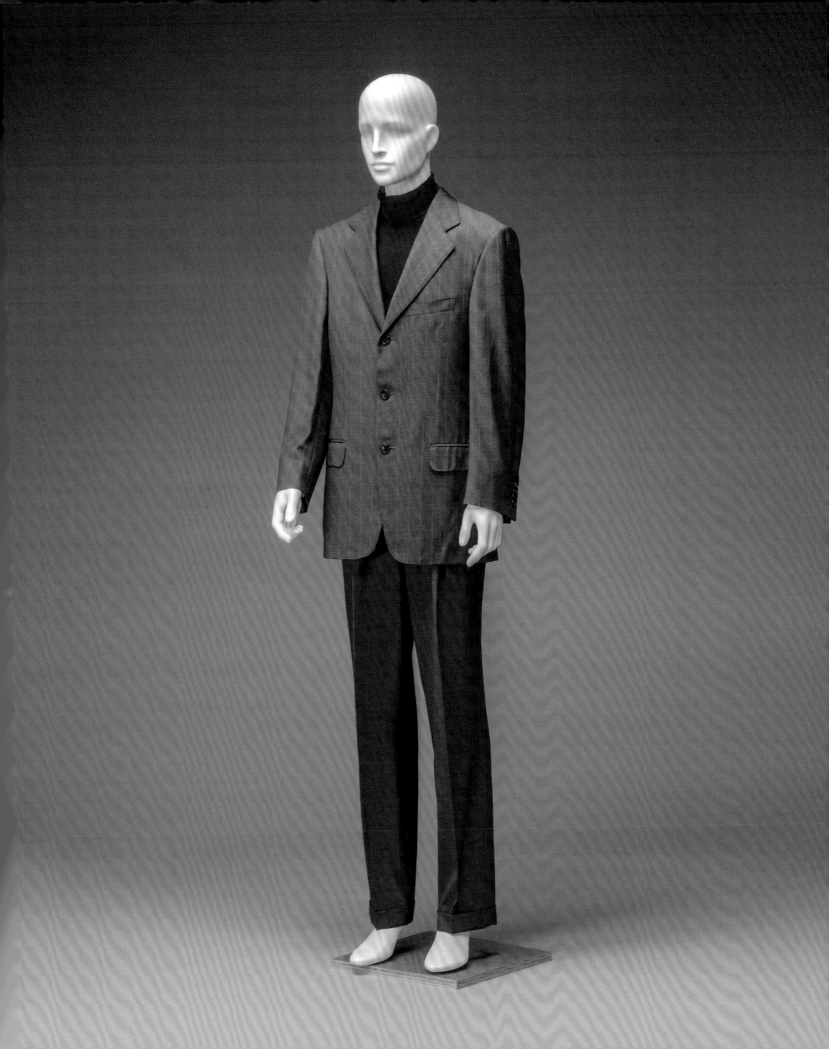

**Norman Norell (United States, 1900–1972)**
Dress, circa 1967
Wool double knit

Gift of Mrs. Lila Mann. 1990.13.2

Balancing an economy of line with the modern short silhouette of the mid-1960s, this cream wool dress is crisp and elegant. It was the creation of legendary New York designer Norman Norell and evokes one of his favorite eras (the 1920s) in one of his go-to materials (wool knit). The Norell "look," as it became known, was achieved through uncompromising and innovative craftsmanship, as beautiful on the inside as the outside. Here, his attention to detail can be gleaned in the clever mirroring of the belt's point with the dip of the front yoke, and the meticulous construction that avoids bust darts (Norell famously thought darts gave a dress a "home-sewn" appearance).

Norman Norell was born Norman Levinson in 1900 in Noblesville, Indiana. He studied at Parsons School of Design and at Pratt Institute, where he graduated in costume design. His professional career began at Paramount Pictures' Astoria Studios in Queens, designing costumes for stars such as Gloria Swanson and Rudolph Valentino. A brief stint working for dressmaker Charles Armour was followed by a move to the firm of Hattie Carnegie in the 1930s. Carnegie was highly regarded for her exclusive garments based on Paris couture models, which she would purchase on twice-yearly trips to France. At Hattie Carnegie Norell was exposed to the most avant-garde Parisian styles, whose cutting, sewing, and fitting techniques he translated into ready-to-wear garments. Later, in 1941, Norell teamed up with wholesale dress manufacturer Anthony Traina to form the Traina-Norell label, often cited as the "Tiffany of the dress industry." Eventually, Norell established his own firm in 1960. The twelve years that followed, until his death in 1972, were Norell's peak design years, in which he achieved a uniquely modern fashion vernacular. As fashion historian Caroline Rennolds Milbank notes, "Norell's 1960s designs are characterized by avant-garde experimentation within the confines of classic American style." LDW

**Unknown maker (United States, 19th century)**
Morning dress, circa 1810–15
Embroidered cotton plain weave

Museum Purchase: Auxiliary Costume Fund. 2009.33.2

In silhouette and hue, this lovely dress reflects the enduring popularity of fashions inspired by ancient Greek and Roman dress which lasted until about 1820. The short cap outer sleeves and wrist-length undersleeves embroidered with lozenges, spots and flowers, and leaf motifs, reflect suitable neoclassical taste, but also suggest that the garment was likely worn as an informal morning dress. Most impressive is the diaphanous cotton, so fine it could be "drawn through a small ring," as the popular adage went. It was the work of the extraordinary spinners and weavers in Bengal, India, who were renowned for centuries for producing the finest of muslins. Fragile and expensive, muslin was labor-intensive to produce and required skilled handwork. Spinning the fine threads was done by women, while men wove the cloth, and it could take up to three months to weave ten yards of the most delicate of muslins, known as mulls.

In the late eighteenth century, the muslin industry was almost completely controlled by the British East India Company, which imposed harsh conditions on and meager remuneration for Bengali artisans. After the War of Independence, the nascent United States developed a flourishing trade with India, with textiles at its core. Between 1795 and 1820, U.S. imports from India surpassed imports from all European nations combined. It was only with the invention of the mule-jenny by Samuel Crompton in 1779 that the English were eventually furnished with the ability to weave muslins of a quality approaching Bengali cloth. The dual inventions of Crompton's mule-jenny and Eli Whitney's cotton gin constituted a turning point in the cotton industry. They initiated the shift in sourcing cotton to the American South, where the forced labor of enslaved Africans would increasingly supply the cotton to the textile mills of Manchester, England. LDW

**Romeo Gigli (Italy, 1949–)**
Frock coat and pants, circa 1988
Linen

Gift of Holly Brubach. 2008.78.1a-b

Romeo Gigli is among the most original fashion designers of the twentieth century. He studied architecture and had little formal training in fashion design, yet seems to have taken a ten-year independent study of global textiles, and an interest in Asian/Oriental styles, from a world tour he embarked on after the death of his parents. Gigli embraced a philosophy of dress that was centered on draping and the feel of the cloth on the body. Favoring clean unfussy lines, he avoided zippers and other sartorial hardware. And while his approach to fashion has been dubbed Japonesque, displaying an affinity with contemporary Japanese designers such as Rei Kawakubo, especially when he first burst onto the fashion scene in the early 1980s, he has dismissed such comparisons.

Unlike his contemporaries in Milan, who were following the trend of big, padded shoulders and bright colors, Gigli's fashions were super-romantic, in the sensual drape of simple fine fabrics of a subdued palette. While fashion houses and designers such as Fendi, Versace, and Gianfranco Ferré showed their collections in a large convention center, Gigli took a more intimate approach to runway presentations, staging them in his atelier, where models wore little make-up and reflected a strong and independent character. As Holly Brubach put it in a *Vogue* profile in May 1988, Gigli's approach was "essentially a refusal—to go along with the tide, to cater to the profligate whims of the people who want to advertise their money, to make a woman into a bright, shiny, be-ribboned illusion, fragile to handle and expensive to maintain."

This ensemble, in cut and textile design, was influenced by menswear of the eighteenth and nineteenth centuries, maintaining a supple and breathable fabric. Like his youthful G line of clothing, it reflects a recognition of societal need for androgynous fashion. AC

**André Courrèges (France, 1923–2016)**
Jumpsuit, ready-to wear, 1970s
Cotton, polyester, acrylic, Lycra

Gift of Myra Gassman. 2018.69.1

André Courrèges, along with Pierre Cardin (see p. 62) and Paco Rabanne, was part of the trifecta of rebellious French fashion designers who rejected the status quo of couture fashions in the 1950s; their work signified the dawn of a new era. A civil engineer by training, Courrèges was always interested in architecture and textile design, and this background—as well as his stint as an Air Force pilot from 1941 to 1945—provided a unique starting point for his career as a fashion designer. When Courrèges moved to Paris, he apprenticed for various design houses before working with Balenciaga for ten years, until he opened his own fashion house, Maison de Courrèges, in 1961.

His meteoric success was based on his ability to both revitalize and preserve high fashion by injecting elements of the youth movement that was going on in London at the time. London-based Mary Quant and Courrèges were the leading figures in introducing the miniskirt to the world in the early 1960s. In 1964, Courrèges, caught up in the zeitgeist of space culture, science fiction, and women's liberation, created the "Moon Girl" look, eliminating most color in favor of stark out-of-this-world white, and including the use of PVC, plastic, A-line silhouettes, goggles, and helmet-shaped hats. The little white dress with colorful trim replaced the little black dress as the frock of choice. He also introduced low-heeled, calf-high "Go-Go" boots made of white plastic, which quickly moved from the catwalk to the dancefloor. His 1965 collection became known as the "Courrèges Bomb." Combined with flat shoes, these clothes liberated women to truly move. His look was boxy, functional, and uncluttered. Moving into the 1970s, his signature looks consisted of clean, sharp, geometrical lines, with minimal decorative ornamentation, often a daisy motif.

The Munich 1972 Summer Olympics staff uniforms were designed by Courrèges. Presenting his first menswear collection in 1973, Courrèges's focus on freedom of movement, comfort, and cut included jumpsuits, which he designed for both sexes. This example may have been influenced by astronaut attire or by racing-car drivers' one-piece garments. AC

**Giorgio Armani (Italy, 1934–)**
Dress suit, early 1990s
Cotton and rayon blend

Gift of Nancy Hariton Gewirz. 2005.98.49a-b

No one has done more to revolutionize the suit than master minimalist Giorgio Armani. In the late 1970s, he loosened its construction, replacing stiff fabrics with softer ones, and removing padding and linings to create jackets that could be worn like shirts, with their sleeves pushed up, balanced by generous trousers that draped the legs. This new male suit—elegant, casual, and sexy—changed the way men dressed. He later applied his rethinking of the suit to women's fashions, where he extended his exploration of reductivist tailoring and softer silhouettes, bringing the masculine innovations into a more fluid, feminine style.

This suit reflects the evolution of Armani's classicism in the early 1990s and features what *Vogue* called two of Armani's trademarks for Spring 1994: "the pajama ease cut of the mandarin jacket and slouchy pants." The jacket is cut loose and boxy, functioning almost as a cardigan, with subtle treatments at the hem, the short standing collar, and the simple patch pockets. The trousers flow loosely on the legs, tapering only slightly at the ankles. The suit steers clear of excess, its understated elegance reaffirmed by the neutral tones of the cotton/rayon-blend fabric, yet it upholds the reputation for craftsmanship that is a hallmark of Italian design, which has helped establish Milan as an important center of luxury high fashion. LDW

**Unknown maker (United States, 19th century)**
Dress, circa 1810
Indigo-dyed printed cotton plain weave

Gift of Jean and Richard Griffith. 2007.72.2

The high-waisted, columnar silhouette of this modest yet charming dress reflects the neoclassical taste in fashion that first appeared in France in the late 1790s. Quickly adopted throughout mainland Europe, England, and America by the early 1800s, it remained popular with subtle variations for almost two decades. The dress features an overall printed pattern of small floral sprigs that was likely the product of the Lancashire textile mills of England, which were entering a period of enormous growth in the first half of the nineteenth century. The distinctive bluish hue was achieved by dipping the fabric in indigo in sequential dye baths, after the small sprigs were first printed with yellow and then mordanted (fixed) with a resist.

Had the dress been made thirty years earlier, the dyestuff would likely have come from the lowlands of South Carolina. In the third quarter of the eighteenth century, South Carolina indigo farms supplied English mills with 80% of this precious dye material, even supplanting higher-quality French and Spanish indigo, and competing with the other major cash crop—rice. Both indigo and, later, cotton were made affordable due to the plantation system and the labor of enslaved people. Yet, indigo production required not just grueling effort, but also skill. Much has been written about the early experiments in cultivating indigo by white plantation owners such as Eliza Pinckney, yet knowledge and expertise in indigo production also came with enslaved people from West Africa, where the dye figured prominently in their own traditional textile arts. By the first decade of the nineteenth century, when this dress was probably made, indigo cultivation in South Carolina had been all but abandoned in favor of a new cash crop— cotton. The American South became the major source of this fiber for the increasingly prosperous textile mills of England and helped fuel Britain's Industrial Revolution. LDW

**John David & Co. (United States, active 1920s–40s)**
Man's formal suit, circa 1934
Wool, silk

Gift of the Mint Museum Auxiliary, bequest of Mildred Gwin Andrews. 1993.24.5a-e

When Elmer Andrews stepped out for the evening in Geneva in 1934, he was clothed in this classic, full evening dress for men, consisting of a fine black wool tailcoat, black wool trousers, white shirt, white vest, and a *de rigueur* top hat. Andrews was in Geneva as a special envoy to the annual summit of the International Labor Organization (ILO) held in June of 1934, and this formal suit was one of three outfits that he wore, along with a dinner suit and a morning suit, which completed the requisite attire for a diplomat in the 1930s. An appointee of President Franklin Delano Roosevelt, who had just implemented his "first 100 Days" of the New Deal, Andrews was to observe the ILO's discussions on improving working conditions around the world and how they might align with Roosevelt's ambitious policies for labor. Andrews was later appointed the first administrator of the Fair Labor Standards Act, which called for minimum wages and work-hour regulations.

Ironically, this formal dress suit is the product of an industry in New York which had its own long history of labor abuse. In the late nineteenth century, the Lower East Side of New York was the mecca of men's suiting manufacture, a trade dominated by German Jewish immigrants, and one of the first to shift to ready-to-wear when sewing machines became widely available. Poor conditions, low pay, and the influx of new waves of immigrants at the turn of the century, especially Eastern Europeans, buoyed the expanding production of men's suiting. From the 1890s to the late 1930s, about half of all manufactured clothing was produced by contractors' shops and home workers. This formal suit was made circa 1934 by John David & Co., a leading menswear clothing company. By then, production had shifted away from the Lower East Side to safer, fire-proof factories, many in the new Garment District of Seventh Avenue. LDW

**Miuccia Prada (Italy, 1948–)**
**Raf Simons (Belgium, 1968–)**
**Peter De Potter (Belgium, 1970–)**
For Prada S.p.A. Italy, founded 1913
Ready-to-wear ensemble: turtleneck with cut-out
circles, oversize sweatshirt with detachable hood,
and skirt, Spring/Summer 2021
Cotton

Gift of Deidre Grubb. 2022.20 a-c

The pared-down serene elegance of classic Miuccia
Prada and the scrappy energetic youth culture
of early Raf Simons combine in this casual chic
ensemble from their Spring/Summer 2021 inaugural
womenswear collection for Prada. Both have been
committed to making fashion for the independent
and confident individual, reflecting contemporary
lifestyles, art, and culture, steering design in new
directions. And they both have developed a sense
of uniform, or essential attire that is part of a basic
individual identity. Their collaborative artistic
leadership was negotiated during COVID lockdowns,
with their first collection conceived and produced
during the pandemic, in a remarkably short period
of time. The fabrics, silhouettes, and aesthetics
came together during a period of pause, reflection,
re-evaluation, and awareness of technology as an
indispensable tool to communicate with each other,
their teams, and their clients.

With the wearer swathed in a luxurious soft, thick
cotton hoodie of an ample cut (a Raf Simons street-
to-chic style) and a historically referenced Prada
pleated A-line skirt, the silhouette is relaxed and
minimal. Minimal, too, is the surface design, with
images and words by frequent Simons collaborator,

artist Peter De Potter. Graphics and symbols address
the multitude of conflicting thoughts about the
quieter life and reliance on technology under COVID.

Conversation and technology were the driving
themes of the S/S 2021 collection. Relying so heavily
on the internet and social media is a part of the
human experience today, and Prada and Simons
engaged the medium more expansively when they
created and communicated their inaugural collection.
Reaching out to a global digital world, they posed
questions to their followers and invited them to ask
questions of the fashion designers. Thus, the S/S
2021 collection represents a convergence of multiple
perspectives in an ongoing conversation between
Miuccia Prada, Raf Simons, Peter De Potter, and
thousands of others. AC

**Franco Moschino (Italy, 1950–1994)**
For Moschino LLC. Italy, founded 1983
"BE SIMPLE!" dress, Moschino Couture,
Fall/Winter 1993
Wool, acetate, rayon

Gift of Rosalie Grubb. 2015.27

Known for relentlessly mocking the fashion system while at the same time profiting from it, Franco Moschino's designs expressed his interests in historic couture, Surrealism, and humanitarian causes through his exuberant surface decorations and impeccable construction. Combining words and iconic symbols—hearts, peace signs, cows, and pearls—his fashions were provocative and fun to wear. Moschino described himself as "half tailor/half artist," and in this dress, we see his brilliance at both. A rare minimalist design, the silhouette gracefully follows the natural contours of a woman's body, in a fine wool fabric of just the right weight to maintain shape and yet permit ease of movement. This is "form follows function" par excellence, and an outstanding example of the superb craftsmanship of Moschino's garments. Here,

he pays homage to one of his favorite couturiers, Gabrielle "Coco" Chanel, with an updated little black cocktail dress. By emblazoning the phrase "BE SIMPLE!" Moschino is shouting at us to avoid the excesses of society at a time of extreme conspicuous consumption.

He was a prolific designer, creating his Moschino Couture line, as well as Cheap and Chic, Moschino Jeans, and accessories. The first Moschino men's show debuted in 1986, followed by the Fall/Winter 1987 men's collection, which was modeled by women.

Well known for the use of ironic and thought-provoking phrases in his designs, such as "Waist of Money" embroidered on a jacket in place of a belt, Moschino was sometimes accused of being a rebel without a cause, but he often used his ads to campaign for social justice causes, including the war against drugs, violence, and cruelty to animals, as well as sustainable best practices in the fashion industry. In Moschino's final collection, labeled "Nature Friendly Garment," the designer introduced an Ecouture line made with environmentally responsible materials. This is one of nine fashions by Franco Moschino in the Mint's collection. AC

**Unknown maker (England, 18th century)**
Informal gentleman's waistcoat and coat, 1760s
Wool, silk, gold-washed silver; original linen lining

Museum Purchase: Auxiliary Costume Fund and Exchange Funds from the Gift of Harry and Mary Dalton. 2003.123.4a-c

While the components of men's dress did not change much throughout the eighteenth century, national and regional variations on the theme communicated country of origin and status as men traveled abroad. In England the style in menswear was more relaxed and unfussy, even in the most elegant attire. In an upper-class culture that enjoyed the bucolic splendors of the countryside and life lived outdoors, fashions for men tended to be more practical. Englishmen and their families were depicted in green leafy landscapes, sometimes in hunting gear or other informal finery.

The coat and waistcoat illustrated here are elegant examples of daywear around mid-century. The coat is a type of morning coat, so called because it was usually worn for the morning horseback ride. Providing comfort and ease of movement, the falling collar was less restrictive around the neck, the coat is cut away in the front, and the sleeves are relatively ample, to accommodate the actions of mounting, riding, and dismounting. A distinctive feature of this coat is the mariner's cuff and forearm design. So called because the style originated in naval officers' coats, the vertically oriented design features four buttons with buttonholes decorated with a metallic stylized foliate pattern, encased in a rectangular frame. Similarly, the bright shining metallic-wrapped threads and needle-worked undulating foliate motifs enliven the collar and coat front.

Revealed by the cutaway coat, the waistcoat is a supremely elegant fashion statement. The purple silk ground is a striking foil for the intricate silver/gold-washed embroidered ornamentation. The lyrical motifs are stitched precisely and with fine silk thread. Needlework of this type was costly and reflected the wealth of the wearer. This ensemble is purported to have been a wedding suit, which is possible since, at the time in England, weddings took place in the morning and required informal dress. AC

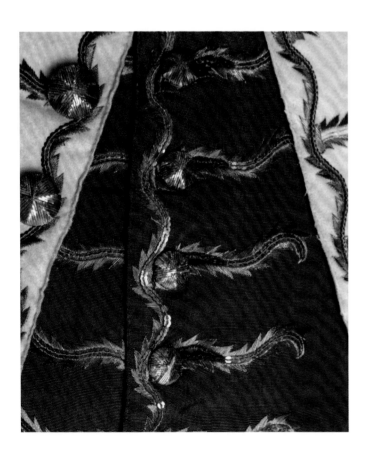

**Geoffrey Beene (United States, 1924–2004)**
Evening dress, circa 1967
Wool, silk satin

Gift of Mrs. Vernon Scarborough. 1992.59.1

Fashion designer Geoffrey Beene once commented, "the more you learn about clothes, the more you realize what has to be left off"—an ethos that is fully realized in this navy and white evening dress from circa 1967. It features classic Beene trademarks: pared-down lines and inventive combinations of fabrics, seen in the soft dark wool, molded into a deep curve at center front that swoops up on the sides into points, contrasted with sculptural white satin at collar, at cuffs, and extending into a long A-line skirt.

Mr. Beene, as he preferred to be called, rejected trends in favor of timeless dressing as part of a sustained exploration of the relationship between clothing and the body. His almost anatomical appreciation for dressing the human form might reflect his early years as a medical student at Tulane University, a career path encouraged by his family yet abandoned when the call of fashion prevailed. He studied fashion design at the Traphagen School of Fashion in New York and the École de la Chambre Syndicale in Paris, capped by an apprenticeship with haute couture designer Edward Molyneux, where he honed his tailoring skills.

Beene returned to New York and launched his own label in 1963. During his decades-long career he remained an iconoclast among Seventh Avenue designers, opting for the artistic over the commercial in his designs. Innovative construction was at the core of his work, resulting in dresses that were almost architectural and earned him the moniker "the godfather of modern American minimalism." Spiral seams that curved the fabric around the body and novel fabric piecing—triangular and curved inserts that exposed and concealed specific areas of the body—allowed for volume and movement. The results, as seen here, are statuesque elegance and purified geometry. LDW

**Pierre Cardin (Italy and France, 1922–2020)**
Dress, 1967
Wool double knit, vinyl appliqué, metal (fastenings)

Gift of the Mint Museum Auxiliary, Purchase Funds Provided by the Costume Collection
Committee. 1993.5.3

Italian-born Pierre Cardin is one of the three French designers—along with André Courrèges (see p. 46) and Paco Rabanne—who created the radically new, youth-focused, futuristic fashion designs of the 1960s. Cardin stands apart as a maverick, both as an artist and businessman. His genius lay in his perfection of his craft and in his creative vision of what fashion should be, not for today, but for the future. Constructing a garment like a sculpture, he was interested in simple geometric forms that did not follow the form of the body and permitted ease of movement for an ever-active lifestyle. His contributions go beyond the sphere of designing clothes to revolutionizing the Paris couture system, from one entirely focused on haute couture one-of-a-kind luxury items, to the democratization of good ready-to-wear garments sold in department stores and available to the masses "for the Duchess of Windsor and the Concierge/Caretaker." In 1959 he represented his women's collection at Printemps, shocking the Paris fashion elite and leading to his temporary expulsion from the Chambre Syndicale de la Haute Couture.

The avant-garde designer's favorite shape was the circle because, he said, it was infinite and referenced the globe—a metaphor for the world. Intrigued by the idea of a man on the moon, he embraced international exploration as well. Particularly fascinated by Asia, he traveled to Japan in 1958, and in 1961 became an honorary professor at the Bunka Fashion College. Introduced by designer Hanae Mori to model Hiroko Matsumoto, Cardin hired Matsumoto to work for him on the runway, shocking the fashion world again, as the first designer to include women of color among his models.

Displaying Cardin's meticulous tailoring, this dress is typical of his minidresses of the 1960s. Made of a type of lightweight double knit which his company developed, the slightly flared A-line construction is decorated with vinyl appliqué, a material associated with space-age fashion design. AC

**Ralph Rucci (United States, 1957–)**
For Chado Ralph Rucci. United States, founded 1994
Coat, Fall/Winter 2007
Double-faced cashmere wool

Gift of Mrs. William McCormick Blair Jr. 2011.79.6

American designer Ralph Rucci has spent more than four decades creating meticulously elegant clothing for women. His approach has been guided by a sense of thoughtfulness and attention to detail: so much so that he added to his company's name "Chado," a reference to the traditional Japanese tea ceremony, as a reminder of the principles of mindfulness and craft that should guide his work.

These qualities are in abundance in a coat from his Fall/Winter 2007 collection. Made of double-faced cashmere in a muted gray color, its clean lines appear simple at first glance. However, its reductivist elegance belies the complexity behind both the conception and execution. According to Rucci, the collection was inspired by amphibians and, more specifically, by the concept of the spine.

Starting from the spine with the straight grain of the fabric, the cashmere flows around the body without benefit of any side seams, dropping and curving until it turns on the bias, furnishing shape and fit. The perfection of the cashmere's flow around the body is assured through Rucci's innovative triangular insertions, called "articulations," and secured with his novel "worm" stitches. The effect of these complex pattern insertions is subtle, yet evocative of ribs.

The construction of the coat required extensive handwork, an anomaly for a ready-to-wear garment, yet typical of Rucci's work. For that, he relies on the talent of his workroom, a team he acknowledges as artists in their own right. For decades they have understood Rucci's proclivity to create through a laborious process that often begins with hundreds of preliminary sketches until a viable design idea percolates. When asked about this approach, Rucci claims the crystallization of an idea is like "taking dictation from a higher source," with the resulting design, in the end, achieving the sublime. LDW

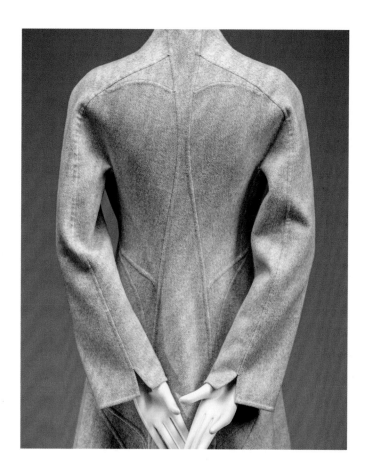

# PATTERN AND DECORATION

Parallel and overlapping themes and variations are abundant in the approach to taking a plain cloth and making it into a colorful, pattern- and decoration-rich fashion fabric. Incorporating color and pattern into the weaving process, warp and/or weft threads are tied in bundles and dyed before weaving. Developed simultaneously in different parts of the ancient world, and known commonly as ikat, such processes create patterns with a blurry appearance. Imparting the woven fabric with color and pattern by resist-dyeing, by means of tying off parts of the cloth or using a paste to resist the subsequent dyebaths, results in patterns in white resisted areas of the color-saturated cloth. This textile technique developed in ancient China, Japan, Southeast Asia, Indonesia, India, the Andes, and West Africa. When used in fashion fabrics, these laborious techniques signified political power throughout the centuries. Co-opted by the hippies in the 1960s and '70s to create circular psychedelic patterns on T-shirts, the message was Flower Power. Fashion designers added resist-dyed flourishes to couture, upcycling popular culture.

Decorating fabrics with flat surface designs to clothe the body has been accomplished by hand-painting, printing, or stenciling on textiles that are to be made into garments, or onto the finished piece of clothing. These early techniques were adapted by early twentieth-century designers, who looked to medieval, Renaissance, and Ottoman botanical patterns, and experienced a resurgence in the 1960s. More recently, artisanal machine-printing on silk has enabled complex, curvilinear and vibrant patterns to be made, some reimagining Baroque and Art Nouveau designs, in many colors to communicate joie de vivre.

Embroidery and needlework incorporating beads, sequins, and mirrors, have for centuries added the element of texture to decorative motifs. For centuries Indian embroidered patterns, from floral sprigs to large boteh (aka Paisley) designs, have decorated fine cottons and Kashmiri wool. Appliquéd elements add depth to the overall pattern on the ground fabric of a gown, and further embellishments, such as laces and other trimmings, add opulence and nostalgia.

**William Michael (United States, 1927–2019) and Sandra Michael (United States, dates unknown)**
For Ashanti Bazaar. United States, 1968–2002
Dress, circa 1978
Silk ikat, silk compound weave, pieced
and embroidered

Gift of Ida Crawford Stewart. 1997.83.3

Harlem in the late 1960s was a place of excitement and cultural renaissance. Advertisements celebrating "Black is Beautiful" proliferated in fashion magazines, and African Americans were increasingly exploring their connections to and roots in Africa. This optimism led William and Sandra Michael, who had no previous experience in manufacturing or retailing, to launch Ashanti Bazaar at 2236 Seventh Avenue in Harlem, where they joined a string of African-oriented shops north of 125th Street. As William Michael noted in a 1972 *New York Times* interview, "Black people were very much together and this type of business had a political meaning... [It was] our personal investigation of African culture."

Ashanti Bazaar featured dresses sewn locally out of colorful African print fabrics, as well as imported African dashikis, djellabas, and tunics. It was a favorite among celebrities such as Kareem Abdul-Jabbar, Betty Shabazz, and Mrs. Jackie Robinson. It was so successful that the Michaels opened a second shop downtown on Lexington Avenue, near Bloomingdale's, where they expanded their inventory beyond African-oriented clothing to include garments and accessories from around the globe.

This exuberantly colorful dress was purchased from the Lexington Avenue Ashanti Bazaar in the late 1970s. A patchwork of patterned fabrics, it features a skirt made with Central Asian silk ikat and a floral brocade, both of which appear again in the long flaring sleeves. The dress is topped with a yoked bodice of maroon velvet pieced with panels of orange embroidery set with mirrors, likely hand-crafted in Kutch, India. The effect is a rich and vibrant mélange of colors and textures.

The importance of both the Harlem and Lexington Avenue boutiques was recognized in 1976 when William Michael received an award for his accomplishments from the Black Retail Action Group (BRAG), an honor he accepted along with groundbreaking African American fashion designers Scott Barrie and Stephen Burrows. LDW

**Zandra Rhodes (England, 1940–)**
"Indian Feathers" dress and bolero, circa 1970
Printed silk chiffon, pleated silk

Gift of Kimberly Kyser. 2002.101.38a-d

For Zandra Rhodes it always started with a sketch. Finding inspiration from many sources—far-flung travels or treasured decorative objects—she made drawings that accrued into a formidable sketchbook which served as the source of her fashion work. Yet her respect for the integrity of the sketch remained. Throughout her career, her garments were shaped around the sketched prints, often resulting in unusual forms, which she dubbed "butterflies."

Rhodes began her formal studies in textile design in 1962 at the Royal College of Art in London, where she encountered other students and future luminaries, such as David Hockney and Ossie Clark. The exciting artistic milieu at the college informed her iconoclastic and multi-disciplinary approach to art, leading to the eventual shift to fashion. She also commenced a lifelong passion for traveling. While in New York in 1970, Rhodes visited the Museum of the American Indian, where she encountered traditional Native American clothing for the first time. In her 1984 book *The Art of Zandra Rhodes*, she recalled: "Faced with the costumes, I was overwhelmed by the sophistication of the cut and the brilliance of the decorative details... Feathers were everywhere; feathers tied on purely as adornment; feathers dyed and sewn with cross-stitch onto jackets; feathers used as edgings which dictated the outline as well as the decoration of clothes." Her sketches from the visit became a collection of four different prints: Indian Feather Sunspray, Feather and Triangle, Indian Feather Border, and Feather Border. They were printed in many colors, including indigo, black, and turquoise, over the years, but made their boldest statement here in this terracotta-red ensemble. The chiffon dress and matching pleated bolero reflect Rhodes's unique approach to manipulating forms to preserve the prints. Shaping around the images, she produces an exuberant radiating pattern that evokes the fluttering of fragile feathers. LDW

**Emilio Pucci (Italy, 1914–1992)**
Dress, circa 1965–70
Printed silk jersey

FIC2008.3a-b

Nobleman, Olympic ski team member, World War II pilot, PhD recipient, politician, and fashion designer: all these were the surprising accomplishments of renaissance man Emilio Pucci. His path to fashion design was through sports, and he showed an affinity for athletics early on. His participation as a member of the Italian Olympic ski team in 1932 led in 1935 to a scholarship to study for a master's degree at Reed College in Oregon in exchange for developing their ski team. Later, an innovative ski ensemble that he had designed for a friend caught the attention of a fashion photographer in Zermatt, leading to an invitation to design skiwear for *Harper's Bazaar* in 1948. The success of that photo spread and his ensembles encouraged Pucci to commit further to fashion design, specifically sleek, modern resortwear.

What soon became Pucci's signature designs—colorful, swirling, abstract, and geometric patterns—were applied first to scarves, then to blouses and dresses. When Marilyn Monroe was captured on film wearing his garments in some of the last photos taken of her before her death in 1962, Pucci became an international success. His iconic designs were perfectly in sync with the trippy, psychedelic looks blossoming in the 1960s, yet were grounded in more conventional sources. Among the eclectic inspirations driving Pucci's designs were Renaissance flags, natural landscapes, and traditional Indonesian and African textiles, made modern through his transformative lines and exuberant color. This dress from the late 1960s features a classic Pucci design of twisting, abstracted florals in shades of green and set against coral red. Printed on his favorite fabric—silk jersey—it exemplifies Pucci's distinctive style, which has kept the brand enduringly popular even today. LDW

## Unknown maker (England, 18th century)
Man's formal coat, waistcoat, breeches,
circa 1760–70
Wool, silk, gold-washed metal, metal-wrapped silk

Museum Purchase: Auxiliary Costume Fund and Exchange Funds from the Gift of Harry and Mary
Dalton. 2003.123.3a-c

Featuring a magnificent skirted waistcoat and
coordinating coat, this formal ensemble boasts a
profusion of elaborate gold trimming and gold-thread-
wrapped shank buttons on fine wool broadcloth
that indicate the suit would have belonged to a
man of considerable wealth, to be worn on special
occasions. The plain minimalist wool fabric,
however, would not have been appropriate dress for
presentation at court; silk, of a solid-color woven type
or patterned weaving, was the prescribed high-status
foundation cloth for applied surface decoration such
as embroidery or lace. This ensemble would have
been completed by a matching pair of breeches,
often missing from collections because they received
wear and tear on horseback, and because they were
sometimes plain and interchangeable with other
ensembles. The breeches seen here are from the
period but not original to the suit.

It is difficult to precisely date formal suits because
such attire was worn infrequently, and styles,
especially in provincial centers outside London,
evolved slowly from 1750 to 1770. The origins of
the man's three-piece suit as we know it in the
West—jacket, trousers, and vest—can be traced
to Charles II, King of Great Britain and Ireland from
1660 to 1685. The padded doublet and hose evolved
into a coat and breeches. Determined to break
free from the dominant French style, the king then
introduced a new component to men's fashionable
dress, creating the waistcoat (so called because it
extended to the waist) and presenting it officially on
14 October 1666. To further distinguish the waistcoat
from French fashion, the preferred fabric was a fine
wool. The choice of wool may have been the court's
effort to bolster the wool industry, as well as to stop
importation of foreign fabrics. However, the king
had little success implementing this initiative, as the
desire for fine silks among the upper classes grew,
coinciding with the arrival of French Huguenots
(Protestants) to the hamlets around Spitalfields,
then outside the bounds of the City of London, after
King Louis XIV issued the revocation of the Edict of
Nantes. Among the refugees were weavers from
Tours and Lyon, the impetus for a major silk industry
in England. AC

### Maria Monaci Gallenga (Italy, 1880–1944)
Wedding dress and train, 1928
Printed silk chiffon, printed cut-silk velvet, metal

Gift of the Mint Museum Auxiliary, donated by Mrs. Thomas Berry. 1983.75.246a-d

Maria Monaci was born into a family of intellectuals in Rome; her father was a professor of philology at La Sapienza, a mentor to both Gabriele D'Annunzio and Luigi Pirandello. Surrounded by her family's art collection and extensive rare book collection, she became fascinated with historic textiles, especially the sixteenth-century *succo d'erba* painted wall hangings.

Following her marriage to Pietro Gallenga in 1903, she was occupied for the next several years with running a household and caring for their three children. Around 1910 she began experimenting with printing on silk textiles. The earliest designs display a distinctive Secessionist look, such as gold stylized wings in a composition inspired by Viennese design. Some of these works were displayed in the *Mostra di architettura*, a companion exhibition to the Roman Secessionist show of 1915. Praise in Rome, Florence, and abroad followed quickly: her fashions were included in the Panama-Pacific Exposition in San Francisco in 1915, and in many others, including the *Exposition internationale des arts décoratifs et industriels modernes* in Paris in 1925. By 1926 she had shops in Rome, Florence, and Paris.

Women's fashion in the first decade of the twentieth century consisted of constraining undergarments, tight-fitting bodices, and long skirts. Interested in bettering the lives of others, Gallenga created modern silhouettes of ample cut and soft silk fabrics, as an antidote to contemporary trends, as artistic dress, or as anti-fashion statements. The cut pattern pieces for these garments were block-printed with medieval- and Renaissance-inspired patterns; Gallenga did not produce yardage. Most of her dresses, capes, and shawls were sold "off the rack," as they were "utopian" dress and one size fit all. She also took commissions, and this rare wedding ensemble was worn by Ellen McClung Berry (1894–1992), an Italophile who wore couture from Rome and Paris. In 1928, McClung married coal magnate Thomas Huntingdon Berry of Rome, Georgia. AC

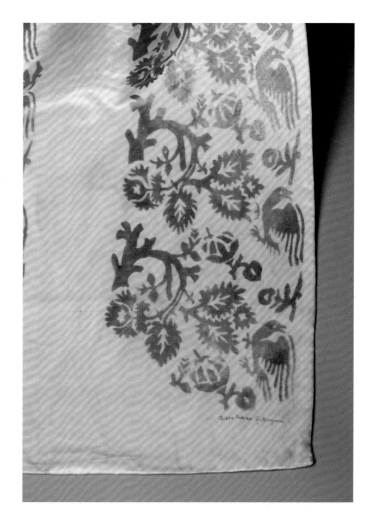

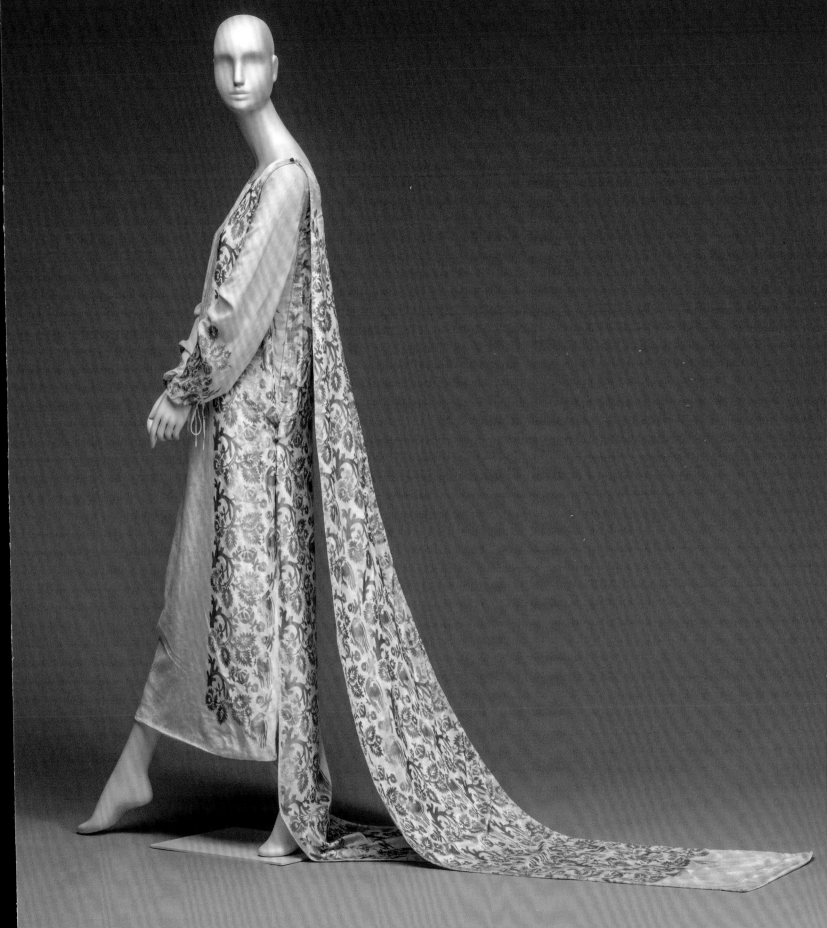

**Alber Elbaz (Morocco and France, 1961–2021)**
For Lanvin. France, founded 1909
Dress, Spring/Summer 2012
Silk, mixed media embroidery

Museum Purchase: Auxiliary Costume Fund. 2012.23

The house of Lanvin was established in Paris in 1909. An immediate success, the company grew to international prominence in the 1920s and '30s, when founder Jeanne Lanvin perfected her signature flair for trimmings, embroidery, and lavish beadwork decoration. Inspired by her rival Gabrielle "Coco" Chanel, she also created a signature perfume, Arpège. Today, Lanvin is the oldest Parisian couture establishment in continuous operation.

Alber Elbaz was appointed artistic director of Lanvin in 2011. Born in Casablanca, he grew up in Holon, Israel, and studied at the Shenkar College of Engineering and Design in Ramat Gan. His career began in the 1980s when he worked for Geoffrey Beene in New York. Moving on to Paris, Elbaz worked for Guy Laroche and was groomed to become head of Yves Saint Laurent ready-to-wear until the business was purchased by the Gucci Group. After a brief stint designing for Krizia in Milan, he returned to Paris to revitalize the couture line for Lanvin.

Carrying on the tradition of designing simple, elegant lines that feature rich surface ornamentation, Elbaz has paradoxically drawn inspiration from historic court dress and world beadwork. The result here is an avant-garde dress that is an encrusted body embellishment, a contemporary woman's suit of armor. This dress caused a sensation when it appeared on the runway as Look #41, lauded as one of the best creations of Elbaz's career. It is an outstanding example of the increased globalization of fashion design in the twenty-first century, when fashion artists from diverse backgrounds are now leading major Paris couture houses and adding their unique training, culture, and lifestyles into the sartorial melting pot. AC

### Anamika Khanna (India, 1971–)

Coat, necklace, pants, Fall/Winter 2019
Thread, bead, and metallic *zardozi* embroidery
on silk faille and cotton

Museum Purchase: Funds provided by Deidre Grubb. 2021.19a-c

Home to more than 1.3 billion people today, India is a geographically, culturally, and religiously diverse society. Mirroring the mosaic of culture are dozens of dress traditions specific to each region. Through color, drape, texture, and imagery, the fashions communicate home state, marital status, social rank, and wealth. The West has imported and drawn inspiration from the fine weavings and printed cottons from India for centuries, and in modern times has modified regional designs of Indian dress to create well-known articles of clothing such as pajamas and the so-called MC Hammer pant.

Each of Anamika Khanna's ensembles exhibits the painstaking detail that she puts into bringing elements of traditional Indian dress into the contemporary design sphere. Her lehengas (ankle-length skirts) and coats, such as the one in this outfit, begin with a solid-color fabric that is embellished with fine hand-embroidered stitches which elevate it to an exquisite example of textile art. In this ensemble, Khanna includes elements such as fringed tassels and luxurious *zardozi* needlework (burnished metal-wrapped-thread needlework that required some 6,000–8,000 hours of labor here), resulting in a sampler of centuries-old techniques native to Indian design. This ensemble is a one-of-a-kind couture marvel. It demonstrates the highest level of surface ornamentation and global design.

Khanna, a self-taught fashion designer, draws inspiration from her Indian heritage, and her designs combine numerous regional techniques to become a collection of the rich history of Indian textile craft and design. Working with makers and workshops from Rajasthan to West Bengal and elsewhere, she devises patterns and handwoven fabrics that combine modern silhouettes and traditional Indian techniques, such as hand-worked thread embroidery, glass beading, and metallic embroidery.

As the first Indian woman to present her designs at Paris Fashion Week and make the Business of Fashion 500 list, Anamika Khanna is a remarkable leader in the growing field of contemporary global design. AC

**Paul Poiret (France, 1879–1944)**
"Ispahan" evening robe, 1907–9
Cashmere, silk

Gift of Louise White Williams. 2010.4.1

This loosely fitted and beautifully embroidered robe exemplifies the modernity and "orientalism" of one of the most visionary couturiers of all time. Paul Poiret is credited with freeing women from the corset, adding color, texture, and opulence to dress, and reimagining pan-Asian garments, sensitively modified with his expert tailoring and attention to French couture detailing. Breaking away from couture dressmaking traditions with numerous pattern pieces, Poiret here appropriated the basic T-shape of a Central Asian Uzbek man's coat, and decorated it with Indo-Persian stylized needlework, to create an ample and striking, three-quarter-length, so-called "caftan" for a forward-thinking woman of the day. Like a cultural anthropologist, Poiret mined world costume and mores, while working in a specific zeitgeist of early twentieth-century aesthetics, from the Wiener Werkstätte to Paris's avant-garde artistic milieu, especially the Ballets Russes. He thus designed clothing inspired by the past, yet completely new and timeless.

"Ispahan" is a rare example of Poiret's oeuvre. Named for the city associated with fine Persian textiles and fashion, this mantle is one of only three known to exist: one is in the collection of the Musée des Arts Décoratifs, Paris, and the other belonged to Denise Poiret, Poiret's wife and muse, and was sold at auction in Paris in May 2005. The "Ispahan" design was published in the album *Les Robes de Paul Poiret racontées par Paul Iribe*, which also featured the designer's "Directoire" collection of dresses, coats, and accessories.

The clothing and lifestyle of Paul Poiret attracted the most famous Parisian actresses of the day as clients, including Gabrielle Réjane and Sarah Bernhardt, as well as the English actress Lillie Langtry. But there were also kindred souls from the United States—including celebrated dancer Isadora Duncan—who sought out Poiret's otherworldly fashions. Helen Emilie Wolf (Mrs. Theodore Rudolf Wolf), who had a dress business in New York before her marriage in 1910, owned this coat and another by Poiret of the same period, also in the Mint's collection. AC

**Halston (Roy Halston Frowick) (United States, 1932–1990)**
**Reiko Ehrman (Japan and United States, 1924–2019)**
Caftan, circa 1970–72
Tie-dyed silk plain weave

From a Southern Collection. 1999.65.69

Before Halston became internationally recognized in the 1970s for his sophisticated minimalist aesthetic, he joined other designers in dabbling in the colorful, exotic styles and forms, such as tie-dye and caftans, that were championed by hippies in the last years of the 1960s. In Halston's hands, however, the Near Eastern caftan was transformed into an elegant yet casual evening gown, a look that suited the jet-set lifestyles of his growing elite clientele. Around 1970, he began collaborating on tie-dyed caftans with Reiko Ehrman, a Japanese artist living in New York. Lesley Frowick, Halston's niece, recalled the collaboration in her 2014 book *Halston: Inventing American Fashion*, noting, "only rarely did he request special designs, for the most part trusting her unique artistry. She'd paint the silk, then bring it to 68th Street."

Reiko had learned the ancient technique of tie-dye (*shibori*) from her mother in Tokyo. Unlike the random, splotchy, tie-dyed patterns made by hippies, Reiko's were carefully controlled and delineated designs produced by a multi-step process that included hand-drawing, painting, and resist-dyeing. She was especially known for producing complicated representational images that were perfectly showcased on the broad surfaces of caftans. Here, the black silk charmeuse pops with otherworldly images of women's faces, along with abstract patches of orange and green tie-dye.

Reiko's success at selling artwork to fashion designers such as Halston spurred a foray into creating garments herself, and she premiered her first collection of ready-to-wear dresses in September of 1976. By then, Halston was already a celebrity on the New York social scene, creating pared-down, casually elegant fashions for the Studio 54 crowd. He would continue to explore the flowing caftan in many new guises and materials, while also starting a craze for a remarkable new fabric—Ultrasuede. LDW

**Mariano Fortuny y Madrazo (Spain and Italy, 1871–1949)**
Mantle, 1919–30
Stenciled silk velvet

Gift of the Mint Museum Auxiliary, donated by Mrs. Thomas Berry. 1985.68.2

While best known for his fashion designs, Spanish-born Fortuny was also an accomplished painter, fabric dyer, printer, etcher, photographer, set designer, and lighting inventor—activities which he explored at his home in Venice. He had relocated there as a boy with his mother and sister after the death of his father, Mariano Fortuny y Marsal, a painter of history and genre paintings. The elder Fortuny had amassed a trove of antiques—decorative objects, historic fabrics, coats of arms, carpets, and garments—that he used as props in his paintings. These collectibles eventually passed to the younger Fortuny and became integral to the interior spaces of Palazzo Pesaro Orfei in Venice, the home that Fortuny and his muse/partner, Henriette Negrin, purchased in 1902.

The palazzo functioned not only as a home, but also as a museum and a creative laboratory for Fortuny and Negrin, with Venice's rich history serving as the incubator. Marcel Proust aptly described how "that inspired son of Venice" had taken the idea of a velvet cape from a Carpaccio painting, "in order to drape it over the shoulders of so many Parisian women."

Renaissance Venice, Florence, and Genoa's textile traditions were Fortuny's inspiration, and he stenciled his sumptuous velvet mantles with classic patterns of pomegranates, palmettes, and stylized floral and vegetal motifs that resembled artichokes or thistles. The richly patterned velvet mantles were often paired with simple, classic "Delphos" dresses (see p. 34).

Here, large-scale tulips are stenciled in gilt pigment onto a cut-silk velvet. The undulating tulip pattern is not Venetian, however, but one of the most recognized of Ottoman designs. Velvets from the Ottoman empire were highly coveted imports in sixteenth- and seventeenth-century Venice, and likely formed part of Fortuny's antique textiles collection in the Palazzo Pesaro Orfei. LDW

## Gianni Versace (Italy, 1946–1997)

Man's ensemble, 1990–95

Silk georgette, raw silk

Charles Mo Collection, given in honor of Jim Craig and Randy Johnson. 2008.27.5.1-2

Armani and Versace were the two powerhouses of Milanese fashion in the 1980s and '90s, and they were complete opposites. Giorgio Armani's fashions were minimal, elegant, and asexual (see p. 49). Gianni Versace's fashion designs defined an era of excess and exuberance, optimism, and prosperity. Unabashedly sexy in silhouette, from haute bordello black to bright colors in flamboyant patterns, often inspired by Italian Baroque sources, his designs reflected a keen sense of art history, from the mainstream to the demi-monde. From Southern Italy, Versace apprenticed with his dressmaker mother before heading to Milan to pursue a career in fashion. From the get-go he brought a fresh new perspective and impacted the use of non-traditional materials in mainstream fashion, such as leather. Rising quickly in the ranks, he established his own brand and presented his first womenswear collection in 1978, followed the next year by a menswear collection—unheard of at that time. Womenswear was the more lucrative sector, and, except for rock stars, menswear hadn't had an aesthetic or sartorial shake-up since the London mod dandyism of the swinging sixties.

In 1990 Versace adopted a new logo, a stylized head of Medusa in a circle. He appropriated the bold, dynamic image from the floor of a Graeco-Roman site in his native Reggio Calabria, drawn to the visual but also to the myth of Medusa as seductress. Approaching menswear with the same intent as with womenswear of accentuating the sexuality and lifestyle of the individual, he created here a shirt that is more like a blouse, with its sheer silky drape and gathered sleeve construction at the cuff. Iridescent bright slim-fit pink pants, in a textured raw silk, were also associated with female attire. Erudite, with an extensive library, and recognized for his achievements by his peers and scholars, Gianni Versace received the Cutty Sark Award in 1988 for being considered "the most innovative and creative designer in the world." AC

**Anna Sui (United States, 1952–)**
Ensemble, Spring/Summer 2022
Silk, polyester, mixed media

Gift of Anna Sui. 2021.81.1-5

Anna Sui is a master at fusing fantasy with fun, and her effervescent Spring/Summer 2022 collection was no exception. Staged among the palms and heady décor of Indochine, a longtime favorite New York restaurant, the show dazzled viewers with its energy and color, transporting them to a quasi-tropical paradise. This ensemble was Look #4, a charming and quirky combination of hot-pink logo T-shirt topped with a sweetly feminine pink mesh-knit dress, a floral-printed pink and gold silk jacket with ballooning sleeves, and a hip daisy-chain water bottle holder, which glided smoothly between references to 1960s Flower Power fashions and contemporary youth culture.

Vintage fashions have often inspired Sui's work, and in a 1992 *Vogue* interview she noted, "my clothes are about nostalgia and memories of my own childhood." Sui was raised in Detroit, Michigan, and moved to New York City in the 1970s, where she studied fashion design at Parsons School of Design, and became friends with fellow student Steven Meisel, and also with designer Stephen Sprouse. The years after graduation were spent working for several sportswear companies, all the while creating her own designs in her own apartment. At the encouragement of friends and several generous supermodels, Sui presented her first runway show in 1991. It was a tremendous success and Sui was awarded the Perry Ellis Award for new talent by the CFDA in 1992.

In the decades following her launch, Sui has continued to present two seasonal runway shows every year and has gained a large and loyal following. Part of Sui's success has stemmed from her eschewing the tradition of extremely expensive fashions in favor of vibrant and whimsical, yet attainable styles. With its beach party-like vibe, the S/S 2022 collection continued that legacy. As one *Vogue* review noted, "This was the designer at her freest and most joyous, and it's certainly about to influence a new generation of Sui girls." LDW

**Oscar de la Renta (Dominican Republic
and United States, 1932–2014)**
Ball gown, Fall/Winter 2013
Silk faille, embroidered with metallic embroidery,
sequins, beads, and pearls

Gift of Oscar de la Renta LLC. 2016.40

"Dazzling," "opulent," and "grand" are words
frequently applied to Oscar de la Renta's
eveningwear, and are particularly appropriate for
describing this dramatic ball gown. The finale piece
of his Fall/Winter 2013 show, its striking purple silk
faille is encrusted with dense silver embroidery,
sequins, beads, and pearls that form a mirror
image of a lone figure on horseback and a tree. The
embroidery sweeps up the front of the dress in a
meandering pattern that covers the bodice and the
narrow sleeves. The large-scale and eye-catching
figure of the rider was inspired by eighteenth-century
toile de Jouy printed textiles, in a historical reworking
that also informed the imagery on several of the
collection's day dresses.

The gown was hailed in the press as a classic Oscar
de la Renta evening dress and typifies the mastery
de la Renta attained after more than six decades in
fashion design. Born in Santo Domingo, he nurtured
his early artistic talent, which led to a career trajectory
spanning two continents and four countries. He honed
his skills at the haute couture houses of Cristóbal
Balenciaga's EISA in Madrid and Lanvin-Castillo in
Paris, before making his move to New York City in
1963. He established his eponymous label in 1965
and quickly became one of the preeminent designers
on Seventh Avenue, producing chic sophisticated
daywear and luxe extravagant eveningwear for an
elite clientele of socially prominent women.

While this gown seems to speak to de la Renta's
signature luxurious style, the F/W 2013 collection also
generated some speculation. Did it perhaps reflect a
bit of the theatrical spirit of then-recently disgraced
John Galliano, who was working at de la Renta as a
"designer in residence" during the creation of the
collection? Like the lone horse rider, the story remains
enigmatic. LDW

**Hanae Mori (Japan, 1926–)**
Evening gown, circa 1970
Printed silk chiffon and viscose

From a Southern Collection. 2000.79.9

Ruffles at collar and cuffs offset butterflies that float across hot pink, blue, and purple stripes in this fluid, ethereal evening dress. A signature work by Japanese designer Hanae Mori, it reflects her brilliance at combining Eastern and Western sensibilities through sensuous fabrics. When she opened her first custom dressmaking salon in Japan in 1951, she had little training in fashion design. Most of it came after her marriage to Kenzo Mori, a textile manufacturer, who encouraged her to explore fabric design and to attend classes at a local dressmaking school. In 1965 she launched her first collection in New York, called "Traditional Beauty of Japan," which showcased the distinctive fabrics she designed herself and produced through her husband's mill in Japan. Subsequent collections included streamlined and flowing A-line dresses, such as this one, which showed off her striking patterns. She also employed printed chiffons one over another to create layers of veiling that moved with soft three-dimensionality.

Four years after Mori's debut in New York, *Women's Wear Daily* reported, "Everyone is talking about these Japanese delicacies, floating butterflies and subtle colors on chiffon, Oriental splendors, marvelous for evening wear no matter what the season." Mori's colors and Japanese motifs—butterflies and stylized waves—melded perfectly with contemporary psychedelic hues and swirling patterns, yet were balanced by her delicate sensibility. The butterfly would eventually become Mori's trademark, and in a 2015 interview at Japanese Fashion Week she recalled, "The butterfly is a symbol of hope which announces the arrival of spring... I chose the butterfly, symbolizing the Japanese woman spreading her wings around the world, as my theme." Success prevailed, and in 1977 Mori opened an atelier in Paris, becoming one of the first Japanese women to be admitted as an official haute couture design house by the Fédération Française de la Couture. LDW

**Jacques Doucet (France, 1853–1929)**
Evening gown, circa 1890
Silk

Museum Purchase: Auxiliary Costume Fund. 1998.13a-b

This unusual and dramatic two-piece evening gown is a marvel of both textile and design. Made of a sumptuous dense dress fabric in a complex construction of satin weave and uncut velvet weave, the genius of the design is in the construction of the bodice and skirt. Arranged to form a bold modern silhouette, the bodice is comprised of four dozen separate pattern pieces, and multiple pattern pieces create the chevron design of the skirt. The gown has been altered at the back, but such changes to original fashion designs are not uncommon and are in fact a part of fashion history. Gowns were modified for successive generations of wearers, or for fancy dress, or by unscrupulous antiquarians.

Jacques Doucet was born into an affluent French family who owned and ran very profitable fabric and clothing businesses in Paris, from the first quarter of the nineteenth century. The Maison Doucet made and sold a wide range of goods, from handkerchiefs to shirts and trousseau items. Inheriting the business in the early 1870s, Doucet transformed it into a couture salon. An erudite, esteemed collector of eighteenth-century art, he channeled a Rococo aesthetic into his hallmark extravagant gowns made of delicate lace, mousseline, satin, and silk. Doucet gowns—especially the tea or at home dresses—are considered masterpieces of the Belle Époque style (circa 1900–14). These, along with tailored suits and fur-lined coats, were very popular among actresses (on stage and off), socialites, and royalty. Paul Poiret (see p. 83) and Madeleine Vionnet also designed for the house. Doucet continued to work until his death in 1929; after his death the house merged with Doeuillet. Doucet's art collection was dispersed to several organizations, and his extensive collections of books and related archival materials on French literature and art history are also now part of prestigious Parisian national institutions. AC

**Walé Oyéjidé (Nigeria and United States, 1981–)**
**Sam Hubler (United States, 1987–)**
For Ikiré Jones. United States, founded 2011
Man's suit: coat, shirt, pants, 2020–2022
Walé Oyéjidé and NFN Kalyan, United States, 1982
Scarf/cape: PIETA. You've Done Your Worst.
And Still We Remain. In Bloom.
Coat: cotton, wool, viscose, silk; Shirt: viscose, cotton;
Pants: viscose, silk; Scarf: silk

Museum purchase: Funds provided by Clay and Deidre Grubb. 2022.18.1-4

Ikiré Jones is a fashion company begun in
Philadelphia by Walé Oyéjidé and Sam Hubler to
bring artistic and finely crafted bespoke menswear
to a wide segment of society. Leaving his work
as an attorney to pursue fashion design, Oyéjidé
sought to make clothes that combined pan-African
aesthetics with European tailoring. After he joined
forces with tailor Sam Hubler, Ikiré Jones—named
for a town in Nigeria and for his wife's family
name—was born.

Very quickly Oyéjidé found his voice in designing
menswear with flair and a message. A gifted visual
artist and storyteller, he used the language of fashion to
clothe a man in confidence and provocative narratives,
ever a reminder of the plight of the disenfranchised.

Fashions by Ikiré Jones have been featured in the
films *Coming 2 America* and *Black Panther*. Walé
Oyéjidé is himself also a musician, writer, global
lecturer, and filmmaker. This ensemble was created
in part for his film *After Migration: Calabria*, in which
the social status of émigrés from Nigeria is upended
in part through their opulent attire, in contrast to
the more mundane dress of the local Italians. It is
emblematic of Oyéjidé's determination to use fashion
to create a more just and empathetic society. The
coat was made for the protagonist—an asylum
seeker who arrives on the seashore near a small
southern Italian town—to wear in the penultimate
scene of the film. Of these fashions, Oyéjidé said,
"The garments evoke a deep history and regality, not
because of their materials and design, but because of
the stories of the persons that have worn them. *After
Migration* employs beauty to illustrate the cultural
gifts that immigrants bravely bear across borders."
The sumptuous fabric pattern is an adaptation of a
Florentine Renaissance artichoke design, the raised
effect the result of a supplementary weave structure.
Pants from a different collection complete the suit.
Draped over the shoulder and tucked into the coat in
a designated Ikiré Jones style, the large silk square
bestows majesty on the wearer. AC

# THE BODY REIMAGINED

Modifications to the body itself have occurred across the globe for centuries, in the form of interventions with the skin, such as tattoos and scarification, as well as topical and less permanent treatments, such as the application of pigment, paint, powder, and make-up, to conform to ideals of identity, health, and beauty. Marking oneself as a member of a certain group, improving health, and making oneself attractive could involve masking or accentuating oneself from head to toe, concealing, displaying, or exaggerating various parts of the body for the pleasure of the self and others. Adding scent, fashionable dress, accessories, and movement completes the self-portrait.

Distorting the natural form, corsets and tight bodices were historically worn by children, men and women, on the one hand to achieve what was deemed to be good posture, and on the other to push flesh up and down to create a small waist and (in the case of women) expose the bosom. The persistence of this constrictive device, in high styles of the twentieth and twenty-first centuries, speaks to both regressive attitudes about body shaping and recurring interest in eroticizing the silhouette.

The lower body was historically accentuated and expanded in a variety of ways. In the West, men's attire until the modern age clothed the leg in tight-fitting hose, exposing full-formed calves. For women, the lower part of the body has long been obfuscated, hidden by layers of underskirts over bum rolls, cage crinolines, or side hoops, increasing girth but decreasing movement. Focusing on the back side, the bustle extended the derrière and the spectator's gaze.

In praise of the artifice of fashion, Charles Baudelaire in the mid-nineteenth century proclaimed an individual inseparable from their attire, maintaining that the excesses of dress mirrored the most beautiful in contemporary society. At the same time, in London and Boston, the Dress Reform Movement rallied against such constrictive clothing as corsets, crinolines, and layers of underskirts. The body clothed has been reimagined, rebelled against, and reinvented throughout history, an ever changing and ever fascinating artform.

## Madame Alix Grès (Germaine Émilie Krebs) (France, 1903–1993)
Evening dress, 1970s
Silk taffeta

Museum Purchase: Auxiliary Costume Fund. 1997.125a-b

The fiery red silk taffeta and voluminous balloon sleeves of this dress command one's attention. Radiating in pleats from the back shoulder blades, the sleeves swell into sculptural lobes, balanced by the straight sheath dress, the austerity of which is relieved only by the long side slit. Not since the previous century—in the 1830s, and again in the 1890s—had sleeves swelled to such proportions. Here, they were the creation of the enigmatic French designer Madame Grès, whose long career engendered admiration but also mystery. Autocratic, determined, brilliant, and austere in her personal habits, she remained secretive about her life and background; even her death was not revealed by her daughter Anne until a year after she had passed away.

She was born Germaine Krebs in the north of France in 1903. She had longed to be a sculptor, but became a sculptor of fabric instead. Working under the name Alix Barton, then later just Alix, she appeared on the Paris fashion scene in the 1930s, establishing a reputation for meticulously pleated silk jersey dresses. Cutting, draping, and pinning the notoriously difficult and liquidy knits herself on wooden dress forms, she developed artful pleated gowns that evoked the draped dresses of ancient Greece, in what was seen as a return to the classical look in the early 1930s.

After the war, she went by the name Madame Grès, an anagram of her husband Serge's name, while continuing to be an innovator well into her elder years. She extended her innate classicism with forays into Eastern-inspired forms such as djellabas, tunics, and saris. In the late 1960s and 1970s, she created a series of silk taffeta dresses featuring striking sculptural sleeves. This dress from the 1970s is modern but almost monastic in its effect, as if the radiating sleeves belong to a futuristic nun's raiments. LDW

**S.A. Carey (United States, active 1870s)**
Reception dress, circa 1878
Silk satin, brocaded, machine lace

Charles Mo Collection, given in honor of Barbara Stone Perry, PhD. 2010.104.2

The extreme artifice of the mid-nineteenth-century cage crinoline (see p. 116) would seem hard to surpass, yet the bustle that followed it in the 1870s extended the excessive volume by shifting it to the rear of the skirt. Flat in the front, with a series of steel cages or horsehair pads in the back, the bustle fastened to the waist and supported a skirt that was often swagged in layers and trimmed with ribbons and fringe. When it first appeared, the bustle was high and full, bursting from the back in a frothy profusion of skirt. By the later 1870s, when this dress was made, bustles were sliding lower and would eventually morph into a fish-tail skirt by the decade's end. Unlike the earlier cage crinoline which hid the lower part of a woman's body in a floating bell shape, the bustle revealed the body in new ways, outlining the thighs and exaggerating hips and buttocks. Combined with a new longer corset that tightly contoured the upper body, the bustle created an undulating, sensual look of softness and rigidity that was understood in its day to be more "natural" but was, in fact, achieved through highly artificial means.

In the 1870s, changes in dress were part of a fashionable woman's daily ritual. This dress, made by S.A. Carey of New York, features rich gold and ivory figured silk and three-quarter sleeves that indicate it was probably worn for a reception or dinner, but not the most formal of events such as balls or operas since those would require plunging necklines and bare arms. The graceful curving neckline opens to form a V-shaped stomacher bodice, while the skirts are drawn up to each side, revealing the underskirt in imitation of a Rococo *Polonaise*, a reflection of the enduring taste for eighteenth-century styles in late nineteenth-century fashion. LDW

**Sadie Nemser (United States, 1886–1966)**
**Joseph Nemser (United States, 1886–1940)**
For Nemser Originals. United States, active
1910s–30s
Afternoon or party dress, 1922–24
Silk crepe, embroidered with silk chenille yarns,
silk ribbon, and glass beads

Gift of the Mint Museum Auxiliary, donated by Lucille D. Withers Ferrell. 1983.75.285

Changes in the way women's dresses were
constructed and worn in the twentieth century
ushered in the modern age, exemplified by the
flapper style of the mid-1920s. In the years leading
up to the emergence of that look, corsets had
become a thing of the past and dresses were
becoming increasingly straight and simple—except
for the appearance of a markedly nostalgic style of
dress known in France as a "robe de style" and in
England as a "picture dress." This full-skirted style
drew heavily on eighteenth-century forms with their
protruding side hoops, called panniers, which lent
a distinctly artificial and horizontal silhouette. This
charming yellow silk crepe afternoon dress is an
excellent example of this look from the early 1920s.
Its simple sleeveless bodice extends into a full skirt,
gathered at the back and hips to allow for a 1920s
version of panniers underneath that would push the
skirt out at the sides.

The romantic effect is enhanced by the dense
floral embroidery in fuzzy chenille, silk ribbon, and
glass beads that embellishes the black silk net inserts
and borders. This hand-embroidery was a hallmark of
Nemser Originals, a husband-and-wife design firm in
New York. Nemser advertised frequently in the *New
York Times* and the trade journal *Women's Wear* as
a creator of exclusive high-end designs which were
to be sold to wholesale dress manufacturers for
copying and mass production. In 1921, the company
made the bold move to eliminate the wholesale
manufacturer, opening its own salon on Madison
Avenue, where Nemser Originals designs were
presented directly to retailers. The firm offered frocks
in the modern slim look, but also dresses such as this
one, advertised in the *New York Times* as the "girlish
silhouette with wide hipline," a style that lasted until
around 1924. LDW

**Iris van Herpen (Netherlands, 1984–)**
"Labyrinthine" dress from "Sensory Seas" collection, Spring/Summer 2020
Laser-cut, heat-bonded, hand-stitched, machine-embroidered silk and glass-organza

Museum purchase: Funds provided by Ann and Michael Tarwater. 2022.22.1

Iris van Herpen is widely admired for her otherworldly but nature-inspired garments constructed through a combination of advanced computer-aided technology and meticulous couture craftsmanship. Combining fashion, art, and science, her "Sensory Seas" collection for Spring/Summer 2020 took inspiration from drawings of the nervous system by the Spanish neuroscientist Santiago Ramón y Cajal (1852–1934) and from marine ecology, especially Hydrozoa, a class of delicately branching organisms. Van Herpen writes, "Shifting between a polypoid stage and a medusa stage, the Hydrozoa embroider the oceans like aqueous fabrics, forming layers of living lace... Colourful meshworks of cellular geometry are translucently layered to create deep-sea aquarelles [watercolors]." About this collection and "Labyrinthine," she states, "'Sensory Seas' holds a microscope over the indelible nuances between the anthropology of a marine organism, to the role of dendrites and synapses delivering infinite signals throughout our bodies... The collection consists [of] 21 silhouettes that illustrate a portrait of liquid labyrinths... The flickers and curves of Cajal's anatomical drawings are revealed in the 'Labyrinthine' technique; 3D lasercut silk dendrites are heatbonded to blossoming leaves of black transparent glass-organza, to then be hand-embroidered onto lasercut pearlescent exoskeletons."

"Labyrinthine" illustrates the philosophy and approach to fashion that make Van Herpen a visionary designer in a category of her own. She evinces the transformative nature of clothing, not only as self-expression but also as a specific type of empowerment that draws from worlds past and future, as well as on the way a dress feels on the body. As a dancer, she is ever conscious of how motion affects emotions, and her choice of materials, whether natural or manmade, is informed by her knowledge of textiles, as well as by her collaborations with scientists and choreographers. Collaboration is key in her methodology, and each collection brings together leading minds from a variety of disciplines, including architects, engineers, scientists, and designers. Recognized internationally for rethinking what fashion means in the twenty-first century, Van Herpen is a guest (foreign) designer in the exclusive Chambre Syndicale de la Haute Couture, Paris, where her fashion presentations at Fashion Week are beautifully orchestrated performances. AC

**Charles Frederick Worth (England and France, 1825–1895)**
**Jean-Philippe Worth (France, 1856–1926)**
For House of Worth. France, 1858–1956
Reception gown, 1895–1900
Silk chiffon, silk satin; needle-worked and
bobbin laces

Museum Purchase: Auxiliary Costume Fund. 2003.126.1a-b

Charles Frederick Worth, founder of the House of Worth, Paris, was known as "the father of haute couture," and a primary force in transforming the French fashion system from a series of independent dressmaking shops into a major international luxury industry. Born in England, from the age of eleven Worth worked for several printing and textile firms, where he gained a thorough knowledge of fabrics and the business of dressmaking. He moved to Paris in 1845 and became a successful salesman and dressmaker, opening his own fashion house, the House of Worth, in 1858. Dominating the fashion scene throughout the second half of the nineteenth century, Worth was known for its gorgeous silks from Lyon and Italy, delicate laces, and trimmings. The house was also the first to employ live models to show dress designs to clients. The interior of the Worth *maison de couture* was decorated like an aristocratic residence, a precious salon where women were pampered by elegantly clad staff and Monsieur himself as they sipped tea. Early on, the Empress Eugénie was Worth's main client, but he dressed women of most every royal court in Europe, as well as wealthy Americans. In 1895, Jean-Philippe Worth, who had assisted his father for decades, became lead designer for the house.

This reception gown displays all the splendor of a House of Worth dress of the *fin de siècle*. Reshaping the body into the fashionable Art Nouveau silhouette, with the monobosom pushed forward through a tight corset and superbly fitted bodice, and the derrière pushed back by means of a cage bustle and layered petticoats, the sinuous S-curve is achieved. The silk-satin-weave foundation of the dress is covered with a sheer silk layer, onto which Alençon and Chantilly lace appliqués combine to create a graceful curvilinear floral pattern. AC

**Romeo Gigli (Italy, 1949–)**
Evening gown, circa 2000
Silk, nylon

Gift of Muriel Kallis Newman. 2005.57

Obscuring the body beneath, this innovative gown is a marvel of concept and construction. The soft sculptural silhouette appears like a cloud of mist surrounding the wearer, masking the armature—a foundation sheath—below. A supple curvilinear length of fabric spirals down the body, and a cascade of net adds a touch of modern glamor to the avant-garde construction. Collapsible, the strapless dress compresses into a circle, to be stored flat in a box.

A radical departure from the neo-Romantic fashion designs of Romeo Gigli in the 1980s and early 1990s, the dress is difficult to assign to a specific designer at the fashion label during this time. While Romeo Gigli's star rose in the second half of the 1980s (see p. 44), when he was cited as the new Armani of the Italian fashion world, there were business troubles with the company and his role as designer waned. And while today it is commonplace for fashion houses to be owned by large conglomerates, it was not so then.

Dramatic and breathtaking, this evening gown was worn by a confident and fashion-forward woman. Chicago art collector Muriel Kallis Steinberg Newman (1914–2008) is best known for the collection of major paintings by Abstract Expressionists and other American modern masters that she amassed with her first and second husbands in the mid-twentieth century. Those works of art, as well as their collections of African and Asian art, were gifted to the Metropolitan Museum of Art. Her fashion collection was equally important, most of which was donated to the Chicago Historical Society. AC

**Unknown makers (England, 18th century)**
Formal dress, sack-back open robe and petticoat,
1760s–80s, altered
Silk, linen

Museum Purchase: Auxiliary Costume Fund. 2009.33.4a-b

Made of an exquisite floral and striped dress fabric, this ensemble is an exceptional example of English aesthetics and high fashion of the Rococo style. Designed and woven in England, the silk textile was made on a draw loom in the Spitalfields area of London, where the finest silk pattern designers, weavers, and other textile workers were located. By the second half of the eighteenth century, Spitalfields had developed into a successful industry catering to an English, Scandinavian, Dutch, and Colonial American clientele. The muted palette and striped and floral pattern reflect the English Rococo, which was more subdued than the French style. English textile designers depicted flowers in a more naturalistic manner than their French counterparts, and the dyers excelled at creating true botanical colors. The texture of the dress silk is achieved through complex weaves, such as *cannelé*, an extended tabby weave with extra warps in which only the wefts move in groups of two or more, creating the ribbed effect of the stripes; the large rose motifs are achieved through brocading or weft floats; and the quintessentially English honeysuckle motif is rendered in the *liseré* effects of the white silk warp threads.

Fashion fabrics were overt symbols of wealth, and such a style of dress allowed for large panels of textiles to be displayed on the amplified body. In this instance, panniers, an undergarment that extended the hips and flattened the front of the body, allowed for the nearly fourteen yards of fabric to be seen and admired. Elegant Rococo excess is accentuated by the appliquéd elements, double-ruffle embroidered-lace sleeve engageants, and fly fringe. The sack back is constructed of box pleats stitched down from the neckband to the shoulders, the unstructured opulent fabric cascading to the floor. AC

**Unknown maker (England, 19th century)**
Wedding dress, circa 1860–65
Cotton plain weave, embroidered, silk satin ribbon

Museum Purchase: Funds Provided by Lyn Mack. 2000.32.1.1-7

Dress in the mid-nineteenth century was defined by notions of correctness and suitability, and nothing expressed this more than wedding dresses. By the 1860s, when this one was made, white had been firmly established as the appropriate color for brides. The stiff sheer white cotton of this dress, known as tarlatan, forms a one-piece garment with fashionable sloping shoulders, gathered puffed sleeves, and an apron overskirt and pelerine cape, trimmed with ivory satin ribbon and fringe in the appropriate current taste.

The enormously full skirt, possibly five yards in circumference, contributed to the hour-glass silhouette, considered the ideal female shape in this period. This shape could not have been achieved without the architectural understructure provided by the corset and crinoline. In the 1860s, both undergarments had been improved by advances in steel technology. Flexible steel boning replaced the whalebone used for centuries to stiffen women's corsets and control their torsos. Likewise, the production of flexible steel springs allowed the new "cage crinoline"—a lightweight skirt of steel rings on tapes—to replace multiple layers of heavy starched petticoats, thus liberating the legs. The cage crinoline was not only modern, but also strong, allowing skirts to swell in size and reach their widest in the early 1860s. The mass production of corsets and the new cage crinolines also made them affordable, even to the lower classes, and they became two of the earliest democratic fashion items.

This all occurred at a time of profound social change in the nineteenth century, the result of urbanization and industrialization that saw the rise of a prosperous middle class clamoring for the outward signs of social legitimization embodied by fashion. While social mores became more complex, compounded by notions of domesticity and virtue, women in the early 1860s were literally occupying monumental amounts of space in a complicated assertion of presence and material display. LDW

**Unknown maker (Europe, 19th century)**
Woman's formal dress, circa 1836
Silk, satin weave with discontinuous supplementary pattern wefts

Museum Purchase: Auxiliary Costume Fund. 2003.126.2

The second quarter of the nineteenth century was a period of inventive and exuberant sleeves. They began to inflate in the late 1820s, developing by 1830 into enormous gigot or "leg-o-mutton" balloons supported inside by down pillows, a silhouette balanced by widening skirts. The charming double-puff sleeves on this dress indicate the later evolution of those sleeves around 1836, when the balloons deflated and formed artful shapes lower down on the arm.

Creating these fantastic sleeves required the clever use of complicated pattern pieces which drew heavily on historical models. Slashed or puffed sleeves in fanciful Renaissance or seventeenth-century styles proliferated, along with "Van Dyke" pointed sleeve edges, collar ruffs, and berthas "à la Puritan," and reflected the Romantic craze sweeping across Europe and America in the second and third decades of the nineteenth century. A reaction against eighteenth-century Enlightenment reason, Romanticism reveled in the sublime, the mystery of nature, emotion, and sentimentality. This was the era that swooned over Lord Byron's poetry, the adventures of chivalrous knights and fair maidens in Sir Walter Scott's novels, and Mary Shelley's Frankenstein, and clothing became one of the most visible expressions of Romanticism's fantasy and historicism.

Here, the luxurious red silk satin is brocaded in a small pattern repeat of lily of the valley flowers in black and cream. The effect is rich and jewel-like. The short sleeves, leaving arms and shoulders bare, indicate the dress was most likely worn for an evening event and would have required suitable gloves, a fan, and one of the imaginatively constructed hairstyles of the period. The dropped puffed sleeves and long full skirts formed by cartridge pleats also foreshadow the elongating of the silhouette that would come with more restrained styles of the early Victorian period soon to follow. LDW

**Yohji Yamamoto (Japan, 1943–)**
Ensemble, Fall/Winter 1995–96
Wool, mohair, nylon, cotton, synthetics

Gift of Deidre and Clay Grubb. 2021.8a-e

When the Japanese fashion designers Yohji Yamamoto and Rei Kawakubo first presented at the Paris runway shows in 1981, they were both revered and reviled. Eschewing the pervasive Western approach to clothing women in formal restrictive attire that accentuated body parts—breasts, waist, derrière—and used colorful fabrics and trimmings, objectifying the female sex, the Japanese designers took a more intellectual approach to fashion. Revolutionaries, they sought to loosen the fit and to deconstruct individual garment pieces, to create new forms in which the shapes and fabric dominated, as anti-fashion for a strong, independent, and artistic clientele.

Avant-garde designer Yohji Yamamoto has repeatedly proclaimed his love of women and his intention to honor them with clothing that is luxurious, but respectful of who they are, their spirit or soul, not their physical attributes. At the same time his fashions often express a gender neutrality or ambiguity: for example, he has employed female models for menswear runway shows. To achieve this, he has focused on eliminating color, choosing black, in the finest fabrics, and gathered a talented team of pattern makers and cutters to work closely with him as he has engineered and reimagined the body clothed as architecture in space.

During the 1980s Yamamoto was intentional about inventing a new vocabulary of shapes freed from references to fashion history in the West or to his native Japan, although he utilized exquisite weavings from the Kyoto area in most of his designs. Those fashions were hailed as timeless in their long silhouettes and blackness, soon acknowledged as radical chic with a decidedly dark urban vibe. By the mid-1980s Yamamoto had developed an interest in certain elements of fashion history that exaggerated parts of the female body, perhaps in appreciation of the sculptural as opposed to the erotic. With impeccable craftsmanship, he once again rocked the fashion world with his 1986 bustle ensemble, a design he revisited in the mid-1990s. Here, we see Victorian and Edwardian references in design details such as the bustle and the tailored suit jacket. Yamamoto turns history on its head by putting the bustle in the front and deconstructing the jacket. AC

**James Galanos (United States, 1924–2016)**
"Black Narcissus" dress, Fall/Winter 1957
Printed silk taffeta (*chiné*)

Gift of the Mint Museum Auxiliary. 2019.11

Philadelphia-born designer James Galanos took a rarefied approach to ready-to-wear. Eschewing the licensing practices and mass production of his East Coast Seventh Avenue competitors, he set up shop in Los Angeles, where he quickly established a reputation for luxurious, meticulously crafted garments of a caliber rivaling Parisian haute couture.

Galanos adhered to traditional techniques and used the finest of European fabrics. The *Aleoutienne* taffeta of this cocktail dress was made by Staron, a premier fabric mill in France, which supplied many Parisian haute couture designers. Its floral pattern of daffodils, daisies, irises, lilacs, and crocuses are boldly set against a black ground with a slight blurry effect called *chiné* that was achieved by printing the pattern on the warp threads before weaving it with a thicker weft. It was a technique employed frequently in mid-nineteenth-century gowns, and reflects an important historical influence on fashions of the 1950s. This post-war "New Look" style featured the return of an hourglass silhouette, corseted waist, and long skirt created with extravagant yards of fabric supported by layers of petticoats; it dominated fashion for most of the decade.

Here, Galanos expresses his own inventive take on the New Look. Created for the Fall/Winter 1957 collection, the dress features a *de rigueur* voluminous skirt made with nine yards of fabric, but also an unusual asymmetrical waistline that dips down to a point on the right side, then cuts straight across on the left. Called "Black Narcissus," this winter-season dress is a sophisticated and dramatic contrast of light and dark, flowers against black ground, that might possibly invoke the famous perfume of the same name created in 1910 by Caron, which boasted a heady, exotic combination of florals, sandalwood, and animal musk to suggest nighttime, eroticism, and the *femme fatale*. LDW

**Pierre Balmain (France, 1914–1982)**
Cocktail dress, circa 1960
Silk, metal-wrapped silk

Museum Purchase: Mint Museum Auxiliary Costume Fund. 1997.101.9

Rising like phoenixes from the devastation of World War II, three couturiers are credited with reinstating Paris as the center of the fashion world, with what *Harper's Bazaar* described as the "New Look": Christian Dior, Jacques Fath, and Pierre Balmain. Balmain's distinction lies in glamorous, conservative dresses, with opulent fabrics inspired by Asian art. He studied architecture at the École des Beaux-Arts, but quickly discovered his heart was in fashion design. He found a part-time job with Edward Molyneux, before landing a hands-on design position at Lucien Lelong. There, he worked alongside Dior and Hubert de Givenchy, honing his skills until he set up his eponymous company in 1945.

Family friends Gertrude Stein and Alice B. Toklas were in the front row of his inaugural fashion presentation that year, and their commentary catapulted the young designer to success. Stein wrote a memoir of her experiences with Balmain during the war for the December 1, 1945 issue of *Vogue*. Toklas commented, "suddenly there was the awakening to a whole new understanding of what *mode* really was: the embellishment and the intensification of women's form and charm."

The shape of this magnificent couture dress reflects a return to the exaggerated silhouettes of centuries past. Enlarging the lower half of the body via a wide bell-shaped skirt echoes the mid-nineteenth-century style, while the cinched-in waist and high bust line recall eighteenth- and nineteenth-century corsets. The influence of East Asian art can be seen in the asymmetry of the composition, with the high-waisted bodice swathed in gracefully ruched silk cascading down the left side, and wrapped in black under the bust, giving the appearance of an obi, as well as in the chrysanthemum pattern of the skirt. Balmain designed an entire wardrobe for Queen Sirikit of Thailand for her world tour in 1960, his sketches and drapery of a similar aesthetic. AC

**Donatella Versace (Italy, 1955–)**
For Versace/Versus. Italy, founded 1978
(Versus line launched 1989)
Cocktail dress, circa 2005
Quilted cotton, lined with rayon acetate

Charles Mo Collection, given in honor of the Mint Museum Auxiliary. 2008.27.9

Of all the devices that have altered and extended a woman's body in the past centuries, corsets have had the deepest effect on fashion. Hidden objects, they contoured the body with whalebone or steel boning, curving around breasts, stomach, and hips, leaving a sensual memory etched on the human psyche. And the allure of corsets has not dimmed; their form is continually revisited by fashion designers even today. Here, the spirit and structure of nineteenth-century corsets informs Donatella Versace's sexy cocktail dress. Low-cut and body-hugging in textured quilted cotton, it features a tight corset-like bodice that sets off curves. The faux lacings criss-cross the front, with sides left open featuring ties that flirt with exposure.

While utterly contemporary, the dress also conjures the body-con styles created by Donatella's brother, Gianni (see p. 89), back in the early 1990s. Gianni Versace founded the house of Versace in 1978, and it developed into a premier brand in the 1980s and '90s, renowned for glamorous, super-sexy clothing. A go-to brand for celebrities, Versace made gowns that were staples at red carpet struts, whether in Hollywood or Cannes. After the tragic death of Gianni in Miami in 1997, his younger sister and muse Donatella took the reins of the firm, having already developed the Versus ready-to-wear line. Donatella forged her own glitzy style yet never forgot the essential sex appeal central to the Versace look, which often drew inspiration from corsets. It is a rarity in the design field for a family member to take over a fashion house and keep it thriving, but this is the case with the house of Versace. Donatella has carried the company's brand of sensuality forward for a new generation and clientele with tremendous success. LDW

**Shae Bishop (United States, 1994–)**
"A Swimsuit to Wear While Looking for Hellbenders," 2021
Ceramic, wool, polyethylene braided filament

Portrait photograph by Myles Pettengill, United States
Gift of María José Mage and Frank Müller. 2022.14

Shae Bishop has always been fascinated by salamanders, particularly the hellbender, the largest salamander in North America. In this suit, he combines that interest with his passion for the craft traditions of ceramics and tailoring. Bishop custom-made the suit, as well as the dress form it rests on, according to his own body's measurements; together, they serve as a self-portrait.

About this project he writes the following: "The hellbender: a creature of legendary proportions… Splashing through Kentucky streams in childhood, it was my white whale, my holy grail: always sought, never found. Moving to the Blue Ridge Mountains as an adult, I finally met this grandfather salamander face-to-face. Wading and snorkeling in the cold mountain rivers … I entered the hellbender's world to observe its secret life.

I made this swimsuit to help me in my quest. Taking cues from the garments of the past, it is lined with knit wool, which insulates even when wet. Starting with a white porcelain, I pressed each tile in my fingers, gradually blending in more and more of a nearly black stoneware clay. Light fading below water, stones tumbling smooth in swift currents, I thought of the river and felt amphibian auspices as I worked.

When I slide the suit onto my body, I feel an immediate change. The soft rustle of the tiles, the weight hugging me closely, I feel pulled toward the water. The hellbenders are patient, as they always have been. They walk the stones, draw oxygen through skin folds, feel the light, smell the water. They wait for me."

Bishop has drawn on the design of early twentieth-century men's bathing costumes, as they were called—knitted wool one-piece designs for swimming—for his pursuit of the elusive hellbender. As a second skin, the suit camouflages the body, blending it into the river stones, mud, and ecosystem of the waterscape. AC

**L.P. Hollander & Co. (United States, active 1870–1930)**
Wedding dress, circa 1884
Silk satin, cut velvet, lace

Museum Purchase: Auxiliary Costume Fund. 2003.74a-b

Boston socialite Alice Dexter Fay wore this two-piece dress for her winter wedding to Dr. Walter J. Otis on February 2, 1884. Fashioned out of cream silk satin and cut velvet in a floral pattern of marguerites, symbols of fidelity, the ensemble combines a stylishly tight bodice, graceful standing collar, and deep pointed bodice, with a luxuriously draped bustle skirt flowing into an extended train, establishing it as among the most up-to-date of fashions for 1884.

Fay's wedding dress was probably created in the custom dressmaking workshops of L.P. Hollander & Co., an exclusive Boston clothing emporium offering custom-made and imported garments in the 1880s. It was founded decades before, in 1848, by pioneering entrepreneur Maria Theresa Baldwin Hollander. Described in *Sketches of Boston* as "a well-connected and gently reared" young woman born in New York in 1820, she fearlessly moved her family to Boston and began making custom clothes for little girls when her husband Jacob's business failed. Within a few years she was established on fashionable Washington Street in Boston, adding boys' clothing then women's garments to her offerings. Hollander created stylish adaptations of designs from fashion magazines, such as *Madame Demorest's Mirror of Fashions*, and "the most fastidious and best-dressed of … people were Mrs. Hollander's patrons from the start," recalled her son, Louis Preston Hollander, in *Sketches of Boston*. Her four sons and a son-in-law later joined her business, which officially changed its name to that of her eldest son, L.P. Hollander, in the 1870s.

In addition to founding a successful business, Maria Theresa Hollander was a passionate abolitionist and advocate for women's rights. Even up until the year before her death, she was actively supporting the latter cause, and was instrumental in organizing a lecture series featuring notable orators on women's suffrage, including Mary A. Livermore and Mary Eastman, in 1884. LDW

**Unknown maker (England, 18th century)**
Formal dress, *robe à l'Anglaise* and petticoat, 1780s
Silk, original linen lining

Museum Purchase: Auxiliary Costume Fund. 2003.104

The two most fashionable styles of women's dress from 1720 to 1780 were the sack back or *robe à la Française*, and the *robe à l'Anglaise*, both popular throughout Europe and in the American colonies. Distinguished from the sack-back silhouette (see p. 114), the English design featured a fitted bodice at the back. Both types were vehicles for showcasing fine silk fabrics, in this instance a labor-intensive resist-dyed textile known as *chiné à la branche*, which used a technique originating not in China but in Indonesia, in which warp threads are tied in bundles and dyed successively in different colors, resulting in a soft blurry pattern when woven.

The silk of this dress would have rustled and shimmered as its wearer walked in candlelight. Throughout the eighteenth century, upper-class women moved very intentionally in their finery.

How they stood, comported themselves in conversation, walked, sat, and danced were all learned behaviors through etiquette books, and through dance teachers, who taught children how to pose and move according to the situation and occasion, as well as how to master the minuet. Constricted by rigid stays or a corset, most often laced tightly in the back, women were forced into an erect posture and constrained from leaning forward. By 1780 the corset had become more rounded, though the breasts remained pushed up and were exposed in a plunging décolleté. Underneath the dress, and on top of a linen shift, women wore side hoops or hip extenders, made of whalebone or cane, that were sometimes collapsible to permit ease of sitting or getting in and out of carriages. They were ridiculed by men, since a woman's silhouette was three times larger than theirs, yet side hoops remained *de rigueur*. Dubbed *panniers* in France, because they were shaped like baskets, by the 1780s they were worn only for formal occasions or at court. AC

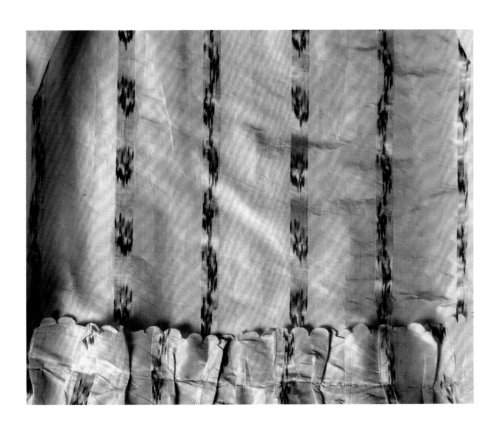

**Oscar de la Renta (Dominican Republic and United States, 1932–2014)**
Ball gown, Spring/Summer 2011
Embroidered silk faille

The Mint Museum Auxiliary's Gift to the Costume Collection. 2011.43a-b

Flowers and a dynamic flamenco-inspired ruffle come together in this apple-green silk faille evening dress and matching pink bolero. From Oscar de la Renta's Spring/Summer 2011 collection, the full-skirted strapless gown is carpeted with sprigs of embroidered carnations and three-dimensional pink appliquéd blossoms. The drama of the dress is echoed in the sculptural pink silk bolero that frames the body in curving ruffles. The effect is retro, ultra-romantic, and feminine; in other words, classic Oscar de la Renta.

Both flowers and ruffles were enduring passions of the designer. The former recalls his birthplace, Santo Domingo, and the intense colors and scent of Caribbean flora. The ruffles speak to his art student days in Madrid, where he was introduced to flamenco culture and the richness of Spanish life. These formative experiences were followed by intense training in haute couture design in Paris, before his eventual move to New York in 1963 and the establishment of his eponymous label in 1965.

This evening ensemble was the finale piece of Oscar de la Renta's S/S 2011 runway show, set to Spanish guitar music. The dress also appeared in the December 2010 issue of *Vogue*, where it was featured in a spread along with seven other de la Renta evening dresses. The provocative photograph by Steven Meisel reinterpreted a famous 1948 Cecil Beaton photograph of Charles James evening gowns, but with a punk twist. Like the original image, the shimmering silk and lace gowns are staged in a formal drawing room awash in pastel tones. Yet Meisel recast the scene using all Asian models with mohawk hairstyles, in a feature on "redefining traditional concepts of beauty." De la Renta's gowns in Meisel's photograph both recall the past and reframe the future, perfectly capturing the spirit of "fashion reimagined." LDW

# SELECTED BIBLIOGRAPHY

Amnéus, Cynthia, Sara Long Butler, and Katherine Jellison. *Wedded Perfection: Two Centuries of Wedding Gowns*. Cincinnati, OH: Cincinnati Art Museum (exh. cat.), 2010.

Arnaud, Claude. *Gabrielle Chanel: Fashion Manifesto*. London and New York: Thames & Hudson, 2020.

Ashmore, Sonia. *Muslin*. London: V & A Publishing, 2012.

Banks, Jeffrey, and Doria de la Chapelle. *Norell: Master of American Fashion*. New York: Rizzoli Electa, 2018.

Bassett, Lynne Z. *Gothic to Goth: Romantic Era Fashion & Its Legacy*. Hartford, CT: Wadsworth Atheneum Museum of Art (exh. cat.), 2016.

Benaïm, Laurence, and Alix Grès. *Grès*. New York: Assouline, 2004.

Breward, Christopher. *The Suit: Form, Function and Style*. London: Reaktion Books, 2016.

Bruna, Denis, ed. *Fashioning the Body: An Intimate History of the Silhouette*. New York: Published for Bard Graduate Center, Decorative Arts, Design History, Material Culture, by Yale University Press, 2015.

Carlano, Marianne. "Maria Monaci Gallenga: A Biography." *COSTUME: The Journal of the Costume Society* 27 (1993): 61–78.

Celant, Germano, Harold Koda, and Giorgio Armani. *Giorgio Armani*. New York: Guggenheim Museum Publications (exh. cat.), 2000.

Coleman, Elizabeth A. *The Opulent Era: Fashions of Worth, Doucet, and Pingat*. New York: Thames & Hudson; Brooklyn, NY: Brooklyn Museum (exh. cat.), 1989.

Crill, Rosemary, ed. *The Fabric of India*. London: V & A Publishing (exh. cat.), 2015.

DeGregorio, William. "Black Narcissus," in *A Catalogue of 20th Century Costume and Textiles*. New York: Cora Ginsburg LLC, 2019.

Eco, Umberto, ed. *History of Beauty*. New York: Rizzoli, 2004.

Ford, Richard Thompson. *Dress Codes: How the Laws of Fashion Made History*. New York: Simon & Schuster, 2021.

Frowick, Lesley, and Liza Minnelli. *Halston: Inventing American Fashion*. New York: Rizzoli, 2014.

Fukai, Akiko, and Tamami Suoh, *Fashion: A History from the 18th to the 20th Century*. Cologne and London: Taschen, 2002.

Goldstein, Gabriel M., and Elizabeth Greenberg, eds. *A Perfect Fit: The Garment Industry and American Jewry, 1860–1960*. Lubbock, TX: Texas Tech University Press, 2012.

Hesse, Jean-Pascal. *Pierre Cardin: 60 Years of Innovation*. New York: Assouline, 2010.

Hill, Colleen, Patricia Mears, Shonagh Marshall, and Valerie Steele. *Reinvention & Restlessness: Fashion in the Nineties*. New York: Rizzoli Electa, 2021.

Jacobs, Laura, and Sirichai. *Beauty and the Beene: A Modern Legend*. New York: Abrams, 1999.

Kennedy, Shirley. *Pucci: A Renaissance in Fashion*. New York: Abbeville Press, 1991.

Koda, Harold. *Goddess: The Classical Mode*. New York: The Metropolitan Museum of Art (exh. cat.); New Haven, CT: Yale University Press, 2003.

Koda, Harold, and Andrew Bolton, eds. *Poiret*. New York: The Metropolitan Museum of Art (exh. cat.); New Haven, CT: Yale University Press, 2007.

SELECTED BIBLIOGRAPHY

Maeder, Edward. *An Elegant Art: Fashion and Fantasy in the Eighteenth Century: Los Angeles County Museum of Art Collection of Costumes and Textiles*. Los Angeles: Los Angeles County Museum of Art (exh. cat.); New York: Abrams, 1983.

McFadden, Mary, Ellen Fisher, and Murray Gell-Mann. *Mary McFadden: A Lifetime of Design, Collecting, and Adventure*. New York: Rizzoli, 2011.

Milbank, Caroline Rennolds. *New York Fashion: The Evolution of American Style*. New York: Abrams, 1996.

Monsef, Gity, Zandra Rhodes, and Ben Scholten. *Zandra Rhodes: A Lifelong Love Affair with Textiles*. Woodbridge, England: Antique Collectors Club, 2005.

North, Susan. *18th-Century Fashion in Detail*. London and New York: Thames & Hudson / V & A, 2018.

Osma, Guillermo de. *Fortuny: The Life and Work of Mariano Fortuny*. New York: Rizzoli, 1994.

Park, Jennifer, Molly Sorkin, and André Leon Talley. *Oscar de la Renta*. Munich and New York: Fine Arts Museums of San Francisco (exh. cat.) and DelMonico Books/Prestel, 2016.

Pastoureau, Michel. *Les Couleurs de nos souvenirs*. Paris: Éditions du Seuil, 2010.

Peck, Amelia, and Amy Elizabeth Bogansky. *Interwoven Globe: The Worldwide Textile Trade, 1500–1800*. New York: The Metropolitan Museum of Art (exh. cat.), 2013.

Smith, Roberta. "Pattern & Decoration: A Movement that Still Has Legs." *The New York Times*, August 5, 2021.

*SS21 Dialogues*. Prada, 2021 (n.p.)

Stanfill, Sonnet. *The Glamour of Italian Fashion Since 1945*. London: V & A Publishing (exh. cat.), 2014.

Steele, Valerie. *Fashion and Eroticism: Ideals of Feminine Beauty from the Victorian Era to the Jazz Age*. New York: Oxford University Press, 1985.

Steele, Valerie. *The Corset: A Cultural History*. New Haven, CT: Yale University Press, 2001.

Sykas, Philip Anthony. *The Secret Life of Textiles: Six Pattern Book Archives in North West England*. Bolton, England: Bolton Museums, Art Gallery & Aquarium, 2005.

Takeda, Sharon Sadako, Kaye Durland Spilker, and Clarissa M. Esguerra, *Reigning Men: Fashion in Menswear, 1715–2015*. Los Angeles: Los Angeles County Museum of Art (exh. cat.); Munich, London, and New York: DelMonico Books/Prestel, 2016.

*Touches d'exotisme, XIVᵉ–XXᵉ siècles*. Paris: Musée de la Mode et du Textile (exh. cat.), 1998.

Trilling, James. *The Language of Ornament*. New York: Thames & Hudson, 2001.

Troy, Nancy J. *Couture Culture: A Study in Modern Art and Fashion*. Cambridge, MA: MIT Press, 2003.

Waugh, Norah, and Margaret Woodward. *The Cut of Women's Clothes, 1600–1930*. London: Faber & Faber, 1994.

Wenders, Wim. *Yamamoto & Yohji*. New York: Rizzoli, 2014.

# ACKNOWLEDGMENTS

The making of any exhibition and catalogue involves planning, fund-raising, research, and conservation of objects and their installation, among other activities. Fashion exhibitions are among the most multi-faceted of projects, in part because of the fragility of the fabrics, the multitude of details related to object-based study due to the complexity of the construction and decoration of the garments, preparing objects for photo shoots, writing and organizing the manuscript, and the labor-intensive process in getting a dress or suit from storage to mannequin, and into the galleries. *Fashion Reimagined: Themes and Variations 1760–NOW* required contributions from many individuals, most of whom worked on these various aspects during the COVID pandemic, remotely or masked, on-site or in other locations.

At The Mint Museum I thank Todd Herman, President & CEO, for his support for this project, and for his commitment to advancing the greater fashion initiative. Jen Sudul Edwards, Chief Curator & Curator of Contemporary Art, since her arrival has enthusiastically championed *Fashion Reimagined* in all phases of production. Former Director of Library & Archives Joyce Weaver responded quickly to many requests. Michele Leopold, Director of Collections & Exhibitions, led and orchestrated a team of staff and contractors who had a hand in most every aspect of the project, with characteristic wisdom and patience. Rebecca O'Malley, Exhibition Coordinator, created and modified schedules and meetings to keep us all on track. Katherine Steiner, Chief Registrar, aka cat wrangler, handled the minutiae involved in preparing garments for study, transport, storage, mannequin challenges, and much more, with the able assistance of Julia Kraft, Assistant Registrar and lead registrar for the exhibition, who took charge of some challenging situations with reason and grace. Rebecca Merriman, former Visual Resources Coordinator, managed the photo shoot book-related image needs. Meghann Zekan, Chief Exhibition Designer, facilitated the design plan with sensitivity and skill. Graphic designer Hailey Bryer enhanced the feeling of the exhibition with just the right fonts and flourishes. Chris Georgalas, Chief Preparator, supervised his team and contributed his talent to the making of the installation. Hillary Cooper, Chief Advancement Officer, herself a fashionista, guided a major fund-raising effort with Amy Tribble, Director of Development, and Martha Snell, Grants & Advancement Coordinator. Clayton Sealey, Director of Marketing & Communications; Cynthia Moreno, Senior Director of Learning & Engagement; Rubie Britt-Height, Director of Community Relations; Maggie Burgan, Program Assistant, Leslie Strauss, Head of Family Programs, and Joel Smeltzer, Head of School & Gallery Programs; Shenilla Smith, Visitor Experience Manager; Amy Smith Grigg, Director of Retail Operations, and volunteers Avery Springs Close Bivens and Donna Anderson, all amazing colleagues, have my gratitude for their roles in this endeavor.

Costume and textile specialist Tae Smith was contracted to carry out conservation surveys and treatments, and as a dresser for both the photo shoot and installation. Looking closely at the historic, modern, and contemporary fashions with Tae over the years yielded much information and many insights, about materials, construction, and alterations. Working together has yielded both sartorial discoveries and fascinating opportunities for future research. She is the silent co-author of this book.

Emily Moore, Vanessa Kassabian, and Andrew Gale of the DLR Group pooled their collective talents to create the mise-en-scène for *Fashion Reimagined*, uniting the disparate sections of the exhibition in a beautiful presentation.

Colleagues in the United States and abroad were generous with their time and knowledge. I am grateful to the following individuals: at the Costume Institute, The Metropolitan Museum of Art, Glenn Petersen, Conservator, Jessica Regan, Associate Curator, and Joyce Fung, Senior Research Associate; at the Victoria and Albert Museum, Susan North, Curator of Fashion 1550–1800, and Silvija Banić, Curator of Textiles before 1800; at the Museum of Fine Arts, Boston, Jennifer Swope, David and Roberta Logie Associate Curator of Textile and Fashion Arts, and the Textile and

ACKNOWLEDGMENTS

Fashion Library; Rebekah Kohan, Global Communications Director, Oscar de la Renta; Michele Majer, Bard Graduate Center; William de Gregorio; Aly Amedei, Unviersity of North Carolina, Charlotte; Marie-Sophie Carron de la Carrière, Chief Curator, Fashion & Textiles, Myriam Teissier, Assistant Textile Conservation, and Emmanuelle Beuvin, Fashion & Textile Librarian, Musée des Arts Décoratifs, Paris; Véronique Belloir, Head of Collections, and Sophie Groissard, Curator in charge of fashions first half of the twentieth century, Palais Galliera, Musée de la Mode de la Ville de Paris. I benefited from conversations with fashion designers Anna Sui, Walé Oyéjidé, Viraj Khanna, Shae Bishop, and Iris van Herpen, as well as Paul van As at IvH.

*Fashion Reimagined: Themes and Variations 1760–NOW* has been discussed with Dan Giles and his team over the course of several years, and their dedication to this project and flexibility with its twists and turns assuaged authors' concerns. This is the second exhibition catalogue that Craft, Design & Fashion has collaborated on with Giles Ltd, and it has been deeply satisfying due to the competencies and collegiality of Allison McCormick, Editorial Manager, as well as Louise Parfitt, Louise Ramsay and Jenny Wilson. Expressing the theme of the exhibition through brilliant book design was accomplished by Ocky Murray.

Producing the content for this manuscript was not a seamless effort, given the COVID pandemic and other factors, and Rebecca Elliot, Assistant Curator of Craft, Design & Fashion, must be singled out for her input in pulling together texts and images, compiling missing information, and accommodating last-minute changes from authors. She did so cheerfully and superbly. Rebecca also took on many CDF responsibilities during my writing "sabbatical."

Co-authors were professional and, despite some pandemic limitations, submitted excellent texts. Fashion icon Anna Sui's prologue set the tone for the book, informative but fun. She has become a dear friend of the Mint, and her generosity of spirit shines through her words. Ellen C. Walker Show, the Mint's Director of Library & Archives, provided a succinct history of the fashion collection at the Mint, and, like a detective, ferreted out new details and stories. Lauren D. Whitley, my partner in crime in writing the catalogue entries, has added much to the understanding of twenty-seven fashion highlights of the Mint's collection, her expertise and new research both object-based and academic. Both on-site at the Mint and through our Friday Zoom sessions, we had scholarly and lively discussions about Minimalism, Pattern and Decoration, and The Body Reimagined.

Moral support is what fuels the excitement for a project of this magnitude, and for their belief in *Fashion Reimagined* I thank Natalie Frazier Allen, immediate past Chair, Board of Trustees; Beth Quartapella, immediate past Chair, MMCDF Collections Board, and Lauren Harkey, Chair, Craft, Design & Fashion Collections Board; Liz Shuford, President, Mint Museum Auxiliary; and my fashion angels, Ann R. Tarwater and Deidre Grubb.

From the mannequins you see on the pages of this book, to the transformative interior architecture of the exhibition, the creation of *Fashion Reimagined: Themes and Variations, 1760-Now* required a multitude of resources. The extraordinary generosity of lead sponsor Wells Fargo Wealth & Investment Management, through Jay Everette, Community Relations Manager, Wells Fargo Social Impact, had huge impact on making the "big idea" reality. The Mint Museum Auxiliary, especially President Liz Shuford, contributed substantially to an exhibition that in fact honors our beloved affiliate group for their role in establishing and building the fashion collection. New kids on the block, Bank OZK, have my heartfelt gratitude for their sponsorship of *Fashion Reimagined*.

**Annie Carlano**


I was fortunate to receive help with my research from many generous friends, colleagues, and scholars. Fashion designer Ralph Rucci was particularly kind in sharing insights into his extraordinary design practice. I am also indebted to my former colleagues at the Museum of Fine Arts, Boston. Jennifer Swope, Associate Curator of Textiles at the MFA, cheerfully accommodated my many visits to the excellent Textile and Fashion Arts library, while Pamela Parmal, *emerita* Chair of Textiles and Fashion Arts, steered me in several good directions. One of these was Philip Sykas, Reader at Manchester Fashion Institute, Manchester Metropolitan University, who generously shared his expertise on the Lancaster textile industry.

At The Mint Museum, Rebecca Elliot, Assistant Curator of Craft, Design & Fashion, and Rebecca Merriman, former Visual Resources Coordinator, fielded my queries with speed and good cheer. A special thanks goes to Sarah Hutcheon at the Schlesinger Library, Harvard University, for kindly facilitating my research there during the limited-access COVID times. I am also most appreciative of the help given by Rebekah Kohan, Global Communications Director at Oscar de la Renta, who stepped up with key information right at the eleventh hour...huzzah! Closer to home, I thank James Moses for his unwavering support of all my endeavors. Finally, to my colleague and friend, Annie Carlano, my deepest gratitude for inviting me to be part of this exciting project.

**Lauren D. Whitley**